WeightWatchers

Spice
up your life ...

over 60 Indian recipes low in points

Cas Clarke

SIMON & SCHUSTER
A VIACOM COMPANY

First published in Great Britain by Simon & Schuster UK Ltd, 2002.
A Viacom Company.

This edition produced for The Book People Ltd,
Hall Wood Avenue, Haydock, St. Helens WA11 9UL

First published 2002
Reprinted 2003

Simon & Schuster UK Ltd.
Africa House
64–78 Kingsway
London WC2B 6AH

Editorial Project Manager: Anna Hitchin
Photography: Steve Lee
Stylist: Jill Davies
Home Economist: Sara Lewis
Design: Jane Humphrey
Typesetting: Stylize Digital Artwork
Printed and bound in China

A CIP catalogue record for this book is available
from the British Library

ISBN 0 743 22057 9

Pictured on the front cover: Chicken Tikka Masala, page 27
Pictured on the back cover: Saag Aloo, page 48

Ⓥ denotes a vegetarian dish and assumes vegetarian cheese and
free-range eggs are used. Virtually fat-free fromage frais and
low-fat crème fraîche may contain traces of gelatine so they are
not always vegetarian: please check the labels.

Ⓥg denotes a vegan dish

contents

your favourite
Indian dishes

At long last the book that all of us who love Indian food but have to count our points have been waiting for! We all know how tempting an Indian takeaway or restaurant menu can be – but we also know how fattening the food is – clearly not a good choice when trying to lose some weight.

In supermarkets, Indian food is now available in "healthy" ranges. However the food that you see displayed on the packaging of these ready-made meals is never quite the same as the dish inside – in looks or in size! Now there is an alternative. This book contains all of your favourite Indian dishes, easy to make and low in points. All of these recipes have been developed to satisfy those whose tastebuds demand yummy, spicy food but want to cut back on fat and calories. Portion sizes will suit even those with big appetites – you'll certainly get more meat, fish and vegetables in these recipes than you will in a similar ready-made meal.

No special equipment is required, however keen cooks may wish to acquire a pestle and mortar so that they can grind their own spices or if you have a food processor you can usually obtain a spice mill for these – I often use a food processor to save time on chopping or grinding. I cook nearly all of my dishes in a non-stick chef's skillet or sauté pan, which comes with a lid and can even be transferred to the oven. Please note that although I have given rough cooking times these will vary with the type of pan you are using and how much heat you are using, so please only use these as a guideline. I often remove the cover of my pan a few minutes before the end of cooking time so that I achieve a curry sauce that I like which for me means the consistency of single cream. You can of course cook the dishes for a few minutes longer to get a thicker sauce.

TOP TIP

The easiest way to cook Indian food is to start by getting out all of the ingredients before you begin cooking. Then preheat your pan while you are preparing the onions or meat. While these are actually starting to cook, measure out all the spices, crush the garlic, grate the ginger and measure out any ingredients that you will be using.

SPICES

In India many different traditional combinations of spices have evolved and these are known as 'masalas'. We know them as 'curry powder' or 'garam masala' spice blend. Try different ones until you find one that is the best for you. I prefer a medium-strength curry powder as these have been developed to enhance the ingredients we use – in India many different ingredients are used. Therefore I prefer to use curry powder as a base ingredient but you can always sprinkle a little garam masala on the finished curry just before serving to add that authentic taste.

No matter what they are called, spice blends contain a mixture of different spices and certain ones are chosen to enhance a particular flavour. These spices can be divided into those that add flavour, character and heat.

FOR FLAVOUR:

Coriander – seeds are used either ground or whole to give a slightly sweet/citrus flavour. The leaves are often stirred into a dish just before serving to add freshness.

Cumin seeds – used ground or whole to give an unmistakable Eastern flavour.

Fenugreek seeds – ground seeds have a slightly bitter taste; they bring out the flavour of other spices.

Garlic – very widely used for its strong flavour.

Poppy seeds – give a nutty flavour.

Turmeric – a root similar to ginger but rarely found fresh here. Ground to a bright yellow powder it adds a bitter flavour to dishes while also adding colour. Beware: it stains!

FOR CHARACTER:

Cardamom – has a unique sweetness. The pods must be slightly crushed before adding.

Cinnamon – use whole or ground to add a woody/sweet essence. If used whole, the stick is not eaten.

Saffron – a strain of edible crocus stamens (not the same as the ones you find in your garden!) An exotic flavour and colour that must be used sparingly.

FOR HEAT:

Black mustard seeds – these are 'popped' in oil to release their hot, pungent, sweet and nutty flavour.

Chillies – widely used in all their forms: dried, ground and fresh. Beware of fresh chilli seeds which will burn your skin; be sure to wash hands thoroughly after contact.

Ginger – Use ground or fresh; if using fresh, you must peel and grate it before use.

Peppercorns – The best pepper in the world is produced in India. Use freshly ground black peppercorns or coarsely ground ones to get the maximum pungency.

OTHER INGREDIENTS

All of these ingredients are now widely available in supermarkets.

Basmati rice – I always specify this rice for Indian cooking as it has a unique delicate flavour; it cooks beautifully without becoming sticky. *1 small uncooked portion (25g/1oz) is* **1½ points.**

Coconut milk – the coconut flesh is ground and pressed to produce this creamy milk. Reduced-fat versions are now available but at the time of writing this book they are still not as widely distributed as they could be. *¼ large can (100 ml) which is 85% fat-free is* **4 points.**

Okra – not always available so you can substitute green beans, however do use okra if you can since it releases a fibrous juice during the cooking process which adds a velvety texture to the dish. Beware: do not use vegetables that have brown markings on the skin since these are past their best.

Tamarind – this used to only be available in specialist shops in a dark, sticky pulp which had to be soaked and strained before use. It is now widely available in larger supermarkets as tamarind paste, which can be spooned out straight from the jar. It gives a unique sour taste. *1 tbsp is 0 Points; 25 g/1 oz is* **½ point.**

Chick-peas – have a nutty flavour and hold their shape well in the cooking process. *1 heaped cooked tbsp (35 g/1½ oz) is* **½ Point.**

Green lentils – strong-flavoured and also retain their shape well. *1 heaped cooked tbsp (40 g/1½ oz) is* **½ point.**

Red split lentils – they cook down to form a lovely soft paste. *1 heaped cooked tbsp (35 g/1½ oz) is* **½ point.**

Yellow split peas – they have a nutty flavour and cook down to a soft cream. *1 heaped cooked tbsp (40 g/1½ oz) is* **½ point.**

Vegetable samosas:
The perfect start to
an Indian meal for
only a ½ point per
serving.

This is a mixture of traditional Indian food and other recipes which have been given a spicy twist. Some you may have come across before, others will be new to you.

VEGETABLE SAMOSAS

POINTS

per recipe: **4**   per serving: **½**

Ⓥ Ⓥg   *Makes 8*
Preparation time: 20 minutes
Cooking time: 15 minutes
Calories per serving: 60
Freezing: recommended

These make a great starter or light lunch. Serve with cucumber raita.

low-fat cooking spray
300 g (10½ oz) diced swede
100 g (3½ oz) diced carrot
4 tablespoons peas
1 teaspoon garam masala
1 tablespoon lemon juice
2 tablespoons chopped fresh coriander leaves
¼ teaspoon dried chilli flakes
4 sheets filo pastry
a pinch of poppy seeds
salt and freshly ground black pepper

1 Preheat the oven to Gas Mark 4/ 180°C/350°F.

2 Using a non-stick pan and the low-fat cooking spray, fry the vegetables for about 5 minutes until lightly cooked but still retaining a little "bite".

3 Take off the heat and add the seasonings. Stir well, and divide into 8 equal portions.

4 Take a sheet of filo and divide it in half lengthways. Spray with low-fat cooking spray. Place a spoonful of filling at the end of a length of filo. Bring one corner over the mixture and then roll the pastry up in a series of triangle shapes until you are left with a small flap of pastry. Spray again and place with the flap underneath the samosa on your baking tray.

5 Repeat with the remaining filo and vegetables.

6 Spray the tops of the samosas with low-fat cooking spray and sprinkle with some poppy seeds.

7 Cook in the pre-heated oven for 12–15 minutes until lightly browned and crisp.

TOP TIP Although this may seem like a lot of mixture, these are best overfilled and then quickly rolled up. Why don't you practice first with a sheet of A4 paper? Cut it in half lengthways and then screw up one half into a ball – use this as the vegetable mixture and practice rolling it up. You'll soon get the hang of this procedure and should be able to do this very easily.

**Dahl soup:
The classic
Indian soup.**

DAHL SOUP

POINTS	
per recipe: 4½	per serving: 2

Ⓥ Ⓥⱖ *Serves 2*

*Preparation and cooking time: 25
minutes*
Calories per serving: 190
Freezing: recommended

Dahl is another word for lentils. This
soup is delicious hot or cold.

100 g (3½ oz) dried split red lentils
low-fat cooking spray
1 teaspoon black mustard seeds
1 medium onion, chopped
*2.5 cm (1-inch) piece of fresh root
ginger, grated*
1 garlic clove, crushed
*1 teaspoon medium-strength curry
powder*
1 teaspoon turmeric
salt and freshly ground black pepper

1 Put the lentils and 500 ml (18 fl oz)
water in a medium-sized saucepan.
Bring to the boil. Cover the pan with
a lid and simmer for 10 minutes.
2 Meanwhile, heat a non-stick frying
pan and spray with the low-fat cooking
spray. Stir-fry the black mustard seeds
until they pop then add the onion
and stir-fry for about 8 minutes until
soft and brown.
3 After the lentils have simmered for
10 minutes, stir in the cooked onion
and all other ingredients then simmer
for 10 minutes more.
4 Pour the mixture into a food
processor or blender and whizz
until smooth, adding a little extra
water if needed.
5 Season to taste and return to a
clean pan to reheat before serving,
or chill until ready to use.

SPICY PRAWN SOUP

POINTS	
per recipe: 1½	per serving: 1

Serves 2

*Preparation and cooking time: 15
minutes*
Calories per serving: 100
Freezing: not recommended

This recipe, adapted from a south
Indian soup, is delicious served as
a starter with chappatis (page 55)
but don't forget to add 1 point
per serving.

1 teaspoon half-fat butter
1 teaspoon Worcestershire sauce
½ teaspoon chilli powder
6 tablespoons tomato purée
600 ml (1 pint) boiling vegetable stock
*100 g (3½ oz) frozen, cooked, large
tiger prawns, defrosted, rinsed and
patted dry on kitchen paper*
salt and freshly ground black pepper

1 Melt the butter in a small saucepan
then add the Worcestershire sauce,
chilli powder and tomato purée.
2 Heat until the tomato purée begins
to splutter, then add 300 ml (½ pint)
of boiling vegetable stock. Stir until
smooth, then add another 300 ml
(½ pint) of boiling vegetable stock.
Simmer gently for 5 minutes, stirring
occasionally.
3 To serve, remove from the heat
and stir in the prawns. Season to
taste then leave to stand for 1 minute
before serving the mixture divided
between two serving bowls.

TOP TIP To ensure that they are
thoroughly defrosted, put the frozen
prawns in a sieve over a small bowl,
covered with a piece of kitchen
paper for at least 2–3 hours.

Spicy Prawn soup: If you love prawns, you'll love this colourful, spicy soup.

Spicy vegetable-topped naan: A satisfying vegetarian meal or ideal on the side of a meat dish.

SPICY VEGETABLE-TOPPED NAAN

POINTS

per recipe: 6½	per serving: 3

V Serves 2
Preparation and cooking time: 20 minutes + making naan
Calories per serving: 315
Freezing: not recommended

Turmeric is used, not only for its flavour, but also for the distinctive golden colour it gives to curries. Serve this very quick and easy curry with naan bread for a light lunch or suppertime snack.

low-fat cooking spray
1 medium red pepper, de-seeded and sliced thinly
1 medium green pepper, de-seeded and sliced thinly
1 medium courgette, cut into 2.5 cm (1-inch) batons
100 g (3½ oz) mushrooms, sliced thickly
4 spring onions, cut into 2.5 cm (1-inch) lengths
1 tablespoon medium-strength curry powder
1 garlic clove, crushed
½ teaspoon turmeric
150 ml tub of 0% fat Greek-style natural yogurt
1½ tablespoons sultanas (about 40 g/1½ oz)
1 naan bread (see page 47 for recipe)
salt and freshly ground black pepper

1 Heat a non-stick frying pan and spray with the low-fat cooking spray. Stir-fry the vegetables for 3–4 minutes, or until starting to soften.
2 Preheat the grill.
3 Add the curry powder, garlic and turmeric to the vegetables in the pan and stir to mix.
4 Reduce the heat and mix in the yogurt and sultanas. Cover the pan with a lid and simmer gently for 2 minutes.
5 Meanwhile, grill the naan bread on both sides.
6 Season the vegetables to taste and serve with the bread.

TOP TIP The vegetable mixture can either be served on top of the naan or the naan can be split in half and the mixture used as a filling.

VARIATIONS These spiced vegetables can also be served as a vegetable side dish with a main course of meat or fish. If served without the naan, the points per serving will be 1.

Any combination of zero-point sliced vegetables that can be quickly stir-fried can be used.

SPICED TUNA

POINTS

per recipe: ½	per serving: ½

Serves 1
Preparation and cooking time: 10 minutes
Calories per serving: 105
Freezing: not recommended

This may look like a lot of ingredients for a quick lunch – but it's easy once you have tried it; you'll want to make it over and over again!

low-fat cooking spray
½ teaspoon black mustard seeds
½ small onion, cut into rings
½ medium green chilli, de-seeded and cut into rings
½ teaspoon medium-strength curry powder
juice of 1 lemon
50 g (1¾ oz) canned tuna in brine or spring water, drained and flaked roughly
1 medium tomato, cut into 6 wedges
½ tablespoon chopped fresh coriander leaves
a pinch of chilli powder
a pinch of sugar
salt and freshly ground black pepper

1 Heat a non-stick pan and spray with the low-fat cooking spray. Add the mustard seeds and heat until they begin to pop.
2 Add the onion rings, green chilli and curry powder. Stir-fry for 1 minute then add half the lemon juice, which will then sizzle and evaporate.
3 Remove the pan from the heat, add all the remaining ingredients and stir gently to mix. Season to taste then serve.

TOP TIP Canned tuna steaks work well in this recipe as they stay in larger chunks than flaked tuna.

VARIATIONS This can be served with a point-free salad as a filling for a medium pitta bread (add 2½ points), or as a topping on 1 medium slice of toast (add 1 point).

TANDOORI PRAWNS

POINTS

per recipe: 4½   **per serving: 2**

Serves 2
Preparation and cooking time: 30
minutes + 2–10 hours marinating
Calories per serving: 135
Freezing: not recommended

16 frozen raw prawns with tails
(200 g/7 oz), shelled and de-veined
(tails still attached), defrosted
salt and freshly ground black pepper
lemon wedges, to serve

FOR THE FIRST MARINADE
juice of ½ lemon
2 garlic cloves, crushed
5 cm (2-inch) piece of fresh root
ginger, grated

FOR THE SECOND MARINADE
4 tablespoons (60 ml) low-fat plain
bio yogurt
1 tablespoon half-fat crème fraîche
juice of ½ lemon
1 tablespoon tandoori blend powder

1 Mix together all the ingredients for the first marinade. Add the prawns, stir well to ensure they are coated, cover and refrigerate for 15 minutes.

2 Mix together all the ingredients for the second marinade.

3 After their first marinade, remove the prawns from the fridge, drain and pat dry with kitchen paper to remove any excess moisture.

4 Add to the second marinade, stir well then cover and return to the fridge for at least 2 hours but preferably 8–10 hours.

5 If using wooden skewers, soak them in water for 10 minutes before using, to prevent them from burning. When ready to cook, preheat the grill or griddle.

6 Shake off any excess marinade and thread 4 prawns on to each of 4 skewers. Season the prawns. Grill or griddle for 5 minutes, turning after 3 minutes, or until the flesh turns completely pinky-white in colour.

7 Serve 2 skewers each immediately with the lemon wedges.

TOP TIPS If you have time, defrost the prawns in the fridge overnight. In the morning rinse them, pat them dry with kitchen paper then add them to the first marinade and leave them for 15 minutes. Drain the prawns, pat them dry with kitchen paper again then add them to the second marinade and leave them all day so they will be ready to be cooked in the evening.

If you cannot find tandoori powder, make your own using 1 teaspoon each of medium-strength curry powder, turmeric and chilli powder mixed together well before use.

VARIATION Make tandoori chicken tikka by substituting the prawns with 2 skinless chicken breasts weighing 150 g (5½ oz) each, cut into bite-size pieces. You will need to cook for 1 minute longer on each side. Using chicken will be 3 points per serving.

ONION BHAJEES

POINTS

per recipe: 2½   **per bhajee: ½**

 Makes 4
Preparation time: 15 minutes
Cooking time: 20 minutes
Calories per serving: 55
Freezing: recommended

This is another cheat's version of a popular starter. Serve two bhajees per person with some very-low-fat yogurt into which you have mixed a little no-added-sugar mint sauce.

low-fat cooking spray
1 onion, sliced finely
2 heaped tablespoons plain white
flour (50 g/1¾ oz)
4 tablespoons water
1 garlic clove, crushed
½ teaspoon turmeric
½ teaspoon ground cumin
½ teaspoon ground coriander
½ teaspoon chilli powder
salt and freshly ground black pepper

1 Preheat the oven to Gas Mark 7/ 220°/425°F.

2 Using a non-stick pan and the low-fat cooking spray, fry the onion for about 8 minutes until very soft and brown.

3 Mix together the other ingredients to form a thick paste – if it is more dough-like add a little more water.

4 Now mix in the onions and stir well.

5 Divide the mixture into 4 equal portions and place each in a non-stick muffin tin.

6 Bake in the pre-heated oven for 20 minutes.

7 Take the bhajees out and turn upside down before returning to the oven for another 5 minutes. Serve warm.

Tandoori prawns:
Enjoy the heavenly
flavours of prawns
with garlic and
ginger in a creamy
tandoori marinade.

1 To make the kebabs, mix together all the ingredients until they reach a sticky consistency.

2 Set aside for 30 minutes to allow the flavours to develop.

3 Preheat the grill.

4 Divide the meat mixture into four equal parts. Form into sausage shapes around four skewers (flatten your kebabs just slightly to make them easier to turn while grilling).

5 Grill under a medium to high heat for 12–13 minutes, turning once. Do not overcook or the meat will become tough. To check the kebabs are cooked through, insert a sharp knife or fine skewer into the meat and press lightly – the juices should run clear.

6 Mix the chopped coriander leaves with the yogurt and serve with the kebabs.

TOP TIP If using wooden skewers, soak in water for 10 minutes before using to prevent them from burning during cooking.

Mixing the kebabs is particularly easy to do using a food processor.

To cook these on the barbecue, cook over a medium heat for about 10 minutes. Turn to ensure that they brown on all sides.

VARIATION You could also use lean minced beef instead of the lamb and save 1 point per serving.

Minced lamb kebabs: These satisfying kebabs are delicious with coriander and yogurt.

MINCED LAMB KEBABS

POINTS

per recipe: 11½   per serving: 3

Serves 4

Preparation time: 10 minutes + 30 minutes marinating

Cooking time: 12–13 minutes

Calories per serving: 115

Freezing: not recommended

These kebabs are easy to make and fun to eat.

250 g (9 oz) lean minced lamb

2.5 cm (1-inch) piece of fresh root ginger, grated

2 garlic cloves, crushed

1 medium onion, chopped finely

1 medium green chilli, de-seeded and chopped finely

½ teaspoon cinnamon

1 teaspoon medium-strength curry powder

½ teaspoon chilli powder

1 tablespoon low-fat plain bio yogurt

salt and freshly ground black pepper

TO SERVE

1 tablespoon low-fat plain bio yogurt

1 tablespoon chopped fresh coriander leaves

EGG SAMBAL

POINTS

per recipe: **5**   per serving: **5**

Ⓥ *if using free-range eggs*
Serves 1
Preparation and cooking time: 25 minutes
Calories per serving: 340
Freezing: not recommended

A 'sambal' is an Indian side dish and this simple, but filling, lunch can be used as a substantial side dish for two people or as a lunch for one.

low-fat cooking spray
2 medium onions, sliced thinly
1 medium egg
30 g (1¼ oz) basmati rice
1 garlic clove, crushed
a pinch of chilli powder
½ tablespoon sultanas
15 g (½ oz) toasted flaked almonds
salt and freshly ground black pepper
fresh green chilli sliced into rings, to garnish (optional)

1 Heat a non-stick pan and spray with the low-fat cooking spray. Stir-fry the onions for about 8 minutes, until soft and brown. Remove from the heat and set aside to cool.
2 Meanwhile, to hard-boil the egg put it in a small saucepan, cover with water and bring to the boil. Simmer for 10 minutes, then transfer to a bowl of cold water. When cool enough to handle, remove the shell and cut into 8 thin wedges.
3 While the egg is cooking, put the rice in a small saucepan. Cover with water, bring to the boil and simmer for 10 minutes. When it is cooked, remove from the heat, drain then cover with a clean, dry tea towel.
4 When everything is ready, mix together the onions, rice, garlic, chilli powder and the sultanas. Season and spoon into a serving dish. Place the wedges of egg around the edge. Sprinkle the rice mixture with almonds and garnish with green chilli, if using.

TOP TIP Covering the cooked rice with a tea towel absorbs the steam from the rice. This prevents the rice from becoming sticky and also helps it to become light and fluffy.

VARIATION To save 1½ points per serving, you could omit the almonds.

MUSHROOM AND CHILLI PÂTÉ

POINTS

per recipe: **1½**   per serving: **½**

Ⓥ *if using vegetarian crème fraîche*
Serves 4
Preparation and cooking time: 25 minutes + 1 hour chilling
Calories per serving: 25
Freezing: not recommended

This lovely pâté can be served in small dishes as a starter for a dinner party, but it is also good as a quickly-prepared lunch, served with either a medium slice of toasted bread or with 4 crunchy crispbreads for 1 extra point each.

200 g (7 oz) button mushrooms, chopped finely
1 small onion, chopped finely
1 medium red chilli, de-seeded and chopped finely
2 tablespoons half-fat crème fraîche
salt and freshly ground black pepper

1 Place all the ingredients in a large saucepan. Stir gently while bringing up to a medium heat.
2 Cover the pan with a tight-fitting lid and leave to cook on a gentle heat for 10 minutes more.
3 Remove the lid and continue to heat, stirring continuously for about 2–3 minutes, until the juices have reduced and thickened slightly. The right consistency is achieved when the thickened juices do not run back when the spoon uncovers the bottom of the saucepan.
4 Spoon into four individual dishes or one large dish. Cover with clingfilm and chill in the refrigerator for at least 1 hour before serving.

VARIATION Use a green chilli instead of a red one and substitute 50 g (1¾ oz) mushrooms with an equal amount of chopped fresh spinach to make mushroom, spinach and chilli pâté. This will not alter the points.

Stuffed aubergine:
A filling and delicious
combination of
vegetables and
spices for only 1
point per serving.

All these curries can be served either as a vegetarian main course or as a vegetable accompaniment to meat or fish. If serving as an accompaniment, the dish will serve double the number suggested – and each serving will be half the points but don't forget to add the points for the dish you are serving it with!

STUFFED AUBERGINE

POINTS

per recipe: 1	per serving: 1

 Serves 1

Preparation and cooking time: 20 minutes
Calories per serving: 205
Freezing: not recommended

Choose an aubergine that it is long and thin rather than fat and thick.

---

25 g (1 oz) dried split red lentils
low-fat cooking spray
1 medium, long, thin aubergine
1/2 medium onion, chopped finely
1/2 medium red pepper, de-seeded and chopped finely
2 medium tomatoes, skinned, de-seeded and chopped finely
1 garlic clove, crushed
1 teaspoon medium-strength curry powder
1/2 teaspoon ground coriander
1/4 teaspoon chilli powder
1 tablespoon tomato purée
salt and freshly ground black pepper

TO SERVE
1/2 tablespoon chopped fresh coriander leaves
1 tablespoon low-fat plain bio yogurt
a pinch of paprika (optional)

1 Put the lentils in a small saucepan, cover with water. Bring to the boil. Simmer for 10 minutes. Drain.
2 Meanwhile, heat a non-stick pan. Spray with low-fat cooking spray. Stir-fry the aubergine, turning frequently for 8 minutes or until soft and covered with browned patches.
3 Remove the aubergine from the pan and set aside to cool.
4 Preheat the grill.
5 Heat a non-stick frying pan and spray with the low-fat cooking spray. Stir-fry the onion and red pepper for about 5 minutes until starting to go soft.
6 Meanwhile, cut the aubergine in half lengthways. Scoop out the flesh using a spoon. Spray each of the hollowed-out aubergine halves with the cooking spray. Grill for about 6–8 minutes until they start to blacken.
7 Roughly chop the aubergine flesh and add it to the fried onion and pepper mixture together with the rest of the ingredients and the lentils.
8 Stir to mix and heat gently until the aubergine skins are ready.
9 Season the fried mixture to taste then spoon into the aubergine skins and grill for 2 minutes. Stir the coriander leaves into the yogurt and serve with the aubergines with a sprinkling of paprika, if using.

TOP TIP To skin tomatoes, place them in a small bowl and cover with boiling water for 30–60 seconds. Remove with a slotted spoon and plunge into cold water. When cool, use a small sharp knife to peel away the skins.

Masala-style
vegetables:
A quick and easy
curry that's
versatile too.

MASALA-STYLE VEGETABLES

POINTS

per recipe: ½   per serving: 0

Ⓥ Serves 2
*Preparation and cooking time: 20
minutes*
Calories per serving: 105
Freezing: not recommended

Try this with saag aloo (page 48)
and a chappati (page 55) for 3½
extra points per serving.

low-fat cooking spray

1 medium onion, chopped

2 garlic cloves, crushed

*2.5 cm (1-inch) piece of fresh root
ginger, grated*

*2 teaspoons medium-strength curry
powder*

½ teaspoon turmeric

½ teaspoon cumin seeds

½ teaspoon chilli powder

100 g (3½ oz) baby carrots

2 tablespoons tomato purée

2 tablespoons low-fat plain bio yogurt

1 tablespoon lemon juice

100 g (3½ oz) baby sweetcorn

100 g (3½ oz) mange-tout peas

salt and freshly ground black pepper

fresh coriander leaves, to garnish

1 Heat a non-stick pan and spray
with the low-fat cooking spray. Fry
the onion for about 5 minutes.
2 Add the garlic, ginger and spices
and stir-fry for 1–2 minutes.
3 Add the carrots, tomato purée,
yogurt, lemon and 100 ml (3½ fl oz)
water. Heat gently until simmering,
then cover with a tight-fitting lid.
Cook for 5 minutes. Add the corn
and mange-tout peas. Cook for
2 minutes.
4 Season to taste then serve garnished
with fresh coriander leaves.

POTATO AND BROCCOLI CURRY

POINTS

per recipe: 9   per serving: 2½

Ⓥ Ⓥⓖ Serves 4
Preparation time: 20 minutes
Cooking time: 20 minutes
Calories per serving: 220
Freezing: recommended

Delicious served with roasted tomato
and chilli chutney (page 51).

800 g (1 lb 12 oz) potato, cubed

*500 g (1 lb 2 oz) broccoli, divided
into florets*

4 garlic cloves, crushed

*2 medium green chillies, de-seeded
and chopped finely*

*1 tablespoon medium-strength curry
powder*

1 teaspoon cumin seeds

2 × 400 g cans of chopped tomatoes

salt and freshly ground black pepper

1 Parboil the potatoes in a large
saucepan for 5 minutes, then drain.
2 Return to the saucepan, add the
remaining ingredients and bring back
to the boil. Cover the pan with a tight-
fitting lid and simmer for 10 minutes.
3 Remove the lid and cook for 2–3
minutes more to reduce and thicken
the sauce.
4 Season to taste then serve.

ALMOND-TOPPED BIRYANI

POINTS

per recipe: $13^{1}/_{2}$ per serving: $3^{1}/_{2}$

 (Vg) *Serves 4*

Preparation time: 30 minutes
Cooking time: 40 minutes
Calories per serving: 340
Freezing: not recommended

Biryani, or biriani, is a Persian word for a type of rice. Traditionally a biryani dish is cooked slowly in an oven. Although rice cooked using this method does not fluff up as it does when boiled, it has a lovely creamy taste.

FOR THE BIRYANI

600 g (1 lb 5oz) mixed zero point vegetables, sliced e.g. cauliflower florets, courgettes, red peppers, small brown mushrooms

250 g (9 oz) basmati rice

550 ml (19 fl oz) vegetable stock

$1^{1}/_{2}$ tablespoons medium-strength curry powder

1 cinnamon stick, broken in half

4 cardamom pods, crushed slightly

1 teaspoon turmeric

1 teaspoon cumin seeds

salt and freshly ground black pepper

FOR THE SAUCE

low-fat cooking spray

2 medium onions, chopped

2 garlic cloves, crushed

5 cm (2-inch) piece of fresh root ginger, grated

2 tablespoons medium-strength curry powder

$^{1}/_{2}$ teaspoon turmeric

$^{1}/_{2}$ teaspoon chilli powder

400 g can of chopped tomatoes

1 tablespoon (10 g) toasted sliced almonds, to garnish

1 Preheat the oven to Gas Mark 4/ 180°C/ 350°F.

2 To make the biryani, mix all the biryani ingredients together in a flameproof, ovenproof dish. Heat gently on the hob until simmering, cover with a tight-fitting lid and transfer to the preheated oven. Cook for 40 minutes.

3 Meanwhile, to make the sauce, heat a non-stick pan and spray with the low-fat cooking spray. Stir-fry the onions for about 8 minutes, until soft and brown. Add the rest of the sauce ingredients to the onions, bring to the boil, cover with a tight-fitting lid and simmer gently for 30 minutes.

4 Put the sauce mixture into a food processor or liquidiser and whizz until smooth.

5 To serve the biryani, fluff up the rice with a fork then scatter the toasted almonds over the top. Serve the sauce separately.

VARIATION You can turn this into a chicken and vegetable dish by stirring in 2 cooked skinless chicken breasts weighing 120 g (4 oz) each, cut into bite-size pieces, just before serving. This will be $4^{1}/_{2}$ points per serving.

Almond-topped biryani: The ideal dish to spice up zero-point vegetables!

GREEN LENTIL CURRY

POINTS	
per recipe: 5	per serving: 2½

Ⓥ Serves 2

Preparation and cooking time: 35 minutes

Calories per serving: 235

Freezing: not recommended

Lentils are very nutritious and often used as a meat substitute in Indian cooking. This curry goes particularly well with the tomato and coriander salad (page 55) for no extra points.

100 g (3½ oz) dried green lentils, soaked overnight then drained

2 teaspoons curry powder

600 ml (1 pint) vegetable stock

low-fat cooking spray

1 teaspoon black mustard seeds

2 medium onions, chopped

2 tablespoons low-fat plain bio yogurt

salt and freshly ground black pepper

1 Put the lentils, curry powder and vegetable stock in a saucepan and bring to the boil. Cover the pan with a tight-fitting lid and simmer for 20 minutes or until the lentils are cooked.

2 Heat a non-stick frying pan and spray with the low-fat cooking spray. Stir-fry the mustard seeds until they start to pop.

3 Add the onions and fry gently for 8–10 minutes until they are soft and deep brown in colour.

4 When the lentils are cooked and the stock has nearly all been absorbed, stir in the yogurt and heat gently.

5 To serve, season to taste then stir the onions into the lentil mixture.

VEGETABLE CURRY WITH FRIED ONIONS

POINTS	
per recipe: 1½	per serving: ½

Ⓥ Serves 4

Preparation time: 20 minutes

Cooking time: 20 minutes

Calories per serving: 110

Freezing: not recommended

low-fat cooking spray

2 onions, 1 chopped and the other sliced thinly

300 g (10½ oz) courgettes, sliced

200 g (7 oz) okra or green beans, trimmed and cut into small lengths

200 g (7 oz) cauliflower, divided into small florets

2 garlic cloves, crushed

5 cm (2-inch) piece of fresh root ginger, grated

1 tablespoon medium-strength curry powder

½ teaspoon ground cumin

½ teaspoon ground coriander

400 g can chopped tomatoes

150 ml (5 fl oz) low-fat plain bio yogurt

1 tablespoon tomato purée

salt and freshly ground black pepper

1 Using a non-stick pan and the cooking spray, fry the chopped onion for 5 minutes to soften.

2 Add the other vegetables except the sliced onion. Cook for 2–3 minutes.

3 Add all the other ingredients except the sliced onion. Season, bring up to a simmer, cover and cook for 20 minutes.

4 Spray a frying pan with cooking spray. Fry the sliced onion on a low heat until soft and very brown.

5 Uncover the curry pan and cook for a few minutes to reduce the sauce.

6 Serve the curry with half of the fried onion stirred through and the other half used to garnish.

CHICK-PEA CURRY

POINTS	
per recipe: 5	per serving: 2½

Ⓥ Ⓥ℮ Serves 2

Preparation and cooking time: 30 minutes

Calories per serving: 240

Freezing: not recommended

Serve with vegetable pilau (page 55) for 4 extra points per serving.

low-fat cooking spray

2 medium onions, chopped

400 g can of chick-peas, drained

2 garlic cloves, crushed

2.5 cm (1-inch) piece of fresh root ginger, grated

1 tablespoon medium-strength curry powder

1 teaspoon cumin seeds

1 teaspoon ground coriander

200 ml (7 fl oz) black tea

1 tablespoon tamarind paste

3 medium fresh tomatoes, skinned and chopped (see Top Tip on page 17)

salt and freshly ground black pepper

green chilli, sliced into rings (optional)

1 Heat a non-stick frying pan and spray with the low-fat cooking spray. Stir-fry the onions for about 8 minutes until soft and starting to brown.

2 Add the rest of the ingredients and heat gently until simmering, then cover the pan with a tight-fitting lid and cook for 10 minutes.

3 Remove the lid and heat for a little longer until the liquid has reduced and thickened slightly.

4 Serve garnished with chilli rings, if using.

TOP TIP Tamarind paste is found beside the spices in the supermarket.

**Chick-pea curry:
A surprising and
delicious dish with
tamarind paste.**

Mixed Vegetables with Coconut: A wonderful combination of slightly sweet and spicy.

MIXED VEGETABLES WITH COCONUT

POINTS	
per recipe: 9	per serving: 2

Ⓥ Ⓥg *Serves 4*

Preparation and cooking time: 30 minutes

Calories per serving: 230

Freezing: not recommended

---

low-fat cooking spray

4 medium onions, sliced

300 g (10½ oz) pre-shredded packet of 'greens' or any leafy cabbage

1 medium red pepper, de-seeded and sliced thinly

1 medium green pepper, de-seeded and sliced thinly

2 × 400 g cans of chopped tomatoes

2 garlic cloves, crushed

5 cm (2-inch) piece of fresh root ginger, grated

2 tablespoons medium-strength curry powder

2 teaspoons ground coriander

1 teaspoon turmeric

4 tablespoons desiccated coconut

6 medium fresh tomatoes, de-seeded and cut into wedges

2 tablespoons chopped fresh coriander leaves

salt and freshly ground black pepper

---

1 Heat a non-stick pan and spray with the low-fat cooking spray. Stir-fry the onions for about 8 minutes until soft and brown.

2 Preheat the grill.

3 Add the greens, peppers, canned tomatoes, garlic, ginger and all of the spices to the pan. Heat gently until simmering, then cover the pan with a tight-fitting lid and cook for 5 minutes.

4 Meanwhile, spread the coconut over a non-stick baking sheet and grill for 2–3 minutes, turning and shaking it to ensure it is browned all over.

5 Remove the lid from the vegetables and cook about 2–3 more minutes to reduce and thicken the sauce.

6 Season to taste then stir in the fresh tomatoes and coriander leaves. Serve sprinkled with the toasted coconut.

VEGETABLE VINDALOO

POINTS	
per recipe: ½	per serving: 0

Ⓥ Ⓥg *Serves 2*

Preparation and cooking time: 25 minutes

Calories per serving: 145

Freezing: recommended

Hot and tasty, as well as sweet and sour this curry is from Goa which lies to the west of India. Serve with 4 tablespoons of cooked plain basmati rice and cucumber raita (page 51) for 3½ extra points per serving.

---

low-fat cooking spray

2 medium onions, chopped

100 g (3½ oz) okra, trimmed and cut into lengths

1 medium red pepper, de-seeded and cubed

1 medium green pepper, de-seeded and cubed

100 g (3½ oz) mushrooms, sliced

2 garlic cloves, crushed

4 tablespoons white wine vinegar

1 teaspoon sugar

1 teaspoon ground cumin

1 teaspoon chilli powder

1 teaspoon turmeric

400 g can of chopped tomatoes

salt and freshly ground black pepper

---

1 Heat a non-stick frying pan. Spray with the cooking spray. Stir-fry the onions for about 5 minutes, until soft.

2 Add the rest of the fresh vegetables.

3 In a bowl or with a pestle and mortar, mix together the garlic, vinegar, sugar and spices to form a paste then add to the pan and cook for 1 minute.

4 Add 100 ml (3½ fl oz) water and the tomatoes to the pan. Cover with a tight-fitting lid and cook for 10 minutes.

5 Remove the lid. Cook for 2–3 minutes more to thicken the sauce.

6 Season to taste then serve.

TOP TIP If you cannot find okra, substitute it with an equal amount of green beans, cut into lengths.

VEGETABLE DHANSAK

POINTS

per recipe: 2	per serving: 1/2

 Serves 4

Preparation and cooking time: 30 minutes

Calories per serving: 105

Freezing: not recommended

Dhansak dishes have Persian origins and are usually quite dry. 'Dhan' means wealthy and 'sak' means vegetables. Serve with fresh mango chutney (page 51) and 4 tablespoons of cooked plain basmati rice which will add 4 extra points per serving.

---

50 g (1³/₄ oz) green lentils, soaked in cold fresh water overnight, drained (see Top Tip)

low-fat cooking spray

1 medium onion, chopped

1 medium courgette, sliced

50 g (1³/₄ oz) fresh okra or green beans, cut into lengths

100 g (3¹/₂ oz) broccoli, divided into florets

---

100 g (3¹/₂ oz) button mushrooms

400 g can of chopped tomatoes

2 garlic cloves, crushed

1 medium green chilli, de-seeded and chopped finely

1 tablespoon medium-strength curry powder

¹/₂ teaspoon cumin seeds

3 medium tomatoes, each cut into 6 wedges

1 tablespoon chopped fresh coriander leaves

salt and freshly ground black pepper

1 Put the green lentils in a medium saucepan, cover with plenty of cold water and bring to the boil. Cook for 10 minutes then drain.

2 Meanwhile heat a non-stick frying pan and spray with the low-fat cooking spray. Stir-fry the onion for about 8 minutes until soft and starting to brown.

3 Add the courgette, okra or green beans, broccoli, mushrooms, canned tomatoes, garlic, chilli, curry powder, cumin seeds and 2 tablespoons of water.

4 Bring to the boil and then cover the pan with a tight-fitting lid and simmer for 7 minutes.

5 Add the green lentils to the simmering vegetables, replace the lid and cook for 5 minutes more.

6 Remove the lid and heat for 2–3 minutes to reduce and thicken the sauce. Season to taste and stir in the fresh tomatoes and coriander to serve.

TOP TIP Although it is not strictly necessary to soak green lentils overnight, doing so reduces the length of time it takes for them to cook.

VARIATIONS You can turn this into a meat curry by replacing the fresh vegetables with 4 skinless chicken breasts weighing 150 g (5½ oz) each, cut into bite-size pieces. Add 150 ml (5 fl oz) cold chicken stock instead of the 2 tablespoons water and cook for 15 minutes before adding the lentils. This will be 3 points per serving.

MARROW, TOMATO AND CAULIFLOWER CURRY

POINTS

per recipe: 5	per serving: 1

 Serves 4

Preparation and cooking time: 30 minutes

Calories per serving: 155

Freezing: recommended

This dish comes from the southern Indian state of Kerala. It makes a satisfying lunch when served with poppadums, adding ½ point per poppadum.

---

100 g (3¹/₂ oz) yellow split peas, soaked overnight in cold water

250 ml (9 fl oz) vegetable stock

1 medium marrow, peeled, de-seeded and cubed

1 small cauliflower, divided into florets

2 garlic cloves, crushed

5 cm (2-inch) piece of fresh root ginger, grated

2 teaspoons medium-strength curry powder

2 teaspoons turmeric

1 teaspoon chilli powder

1 teaspoon ground coriander

¹/₂ teaspoon cardamom pods, crushed slightly

¹/₂ teaspoon cumin seeds

---

1 tablespoon frozen peas

4 medium tomatoes, de-seeded and cut into wedges

1 tablespoon chopped fresh coriander leaves

salt and freshly ground black pepper

1 Put the yellow split peas in a pan. Cover with the vegetable stock. Bring up to a medium heat and then heat for 10 minutes.

2 Add the marrow, cauliflower, garlic and all the spices. Cover with a tight-fitting lid. Simmer for 8 minutes.

3 Add the peas. Cook for a further 3–4 minutes. Add the tomatoes and coriander leaves and season.

CREAMY CAULIFLOWER KASHMIR

POINTS

per recipe: 26   per serving: 6½

 if using vegetarian crème fraîche
Serves 4
Preparation time: 15 minutes
Cooking time: 15 minutes
Calories per serving: 300
Freezing: not recommended

A truly scrumptious, fruity curry – mild but very creamy. If you serve it with roasted tomato and chilli chutney (page 51), the flavours will contrast beautifully, adding no extra points.

low-fat cooking spray

2 medium onions, chopped

5 cm (2-inch) piece of fresh root ginger, grated

2 garlic cloves, crushed

1 teaspoon turmeric

1 tablespoon medium-strength curry powder

1 large cauliflower, divided into florets

2 bay leaves

100 ml (3½ fl oz) half-fat crème fraîche

425 g can of crushed pineapple in juice

2 medium bananas, sliced

200 ml (7 fl oz) coconut milk

salt and freshly ground black pepper

1 Heat a non-stick pan and spray with the low-fat cooking spray. Stir-fry the onions for 4–5 minutes until soft but do not allow to brown.
2 Add the rest of the ingredients. Gently heat until simmering, then cover the pan with a tight-fitting lid and cook for about 12 minutes or until the cauliflower is cooked to your taste.

3 Remove the lid and continue to cook uncovered for about 2–3 minutes or until the sauce has thickened slightly. Check the seasoning before serving.

TOP TIPS If you like hot curries, use green chillies sliced into rings to garnish.

Look out for reduced-fat coconut milk and substitute it for full-fat coconut milk if you can. Unfortunately it is not widely available but if you can find it this dish will only be 4½ points per serving.

VARIATION Substitute half of the cauliflower with 200 g (7 oz) button mushrooms to make a creamy cauliflower and mushroom curry. This will not alter the points.

MUSHROOM CURRY

POINTS

per recipe: ½   per serving: 0

 Serves 2
Preparation and cooking time: 30 minutes
Calories per serving: 95
Freezing: not recommended

Fenugreek is available as a leaf or, more commonly, as a seed which is ground before use. It can have quite a bitter taste and is often used to flavour masalas.

This curry goes particularly well with Bombay-style potatoes (page 52), but don't forget to add on 2 extra points.

low-fat cooking spray

2 medium onions, sliced

300 g (10½ oz) mixed mushrooms, sliced thickly or halved depending on size

2 garlic cloves, crushed

2 teaspoons medium-strength curry powder

½ teaspoon cumin seeds

3 tablespoons tomato purée

4 tablespoons low-fat plain bio yogurt

salt and freshly ground black pepper

½ teaspoon ground fenugreek (optional)

1 Heat a non-stick pan and spray with the low-fat cooking spray. Stir-fry the onions for about 8 minutes until soft and brown.
2 Add the rest of the ingredients to the pan and heat gently until

simmering, then cover the pan with a tight-fitting lid and cook for 10 minutes.
3 Remove the lid and continue cooking for about 2–3 minutes until the sauce has reduced and thickened slightly.
4 Season to taste and serve.

TOP TIP This curry will be a great favourite – if you like mushrooms! Use a mixture of mushrooms, such as Portabello and brown chestnut, as you will enjoy the different textures.

VARIATION To make a mushroom and spinach curry, simply stir in two large handfuls of chopped fresh spinach at step 3, and cook until the spinach has wilted. This will not alter the points.

Creamy cauliflower kashmir: Bananas, pineapple and coconut make this creamy curry taste gorgeous.

Chicken tikka masala: This extremely popular curry does not actually originate in India... but in England!

chicken & other meat curries

In this chapter you will find some of your favourite restaurant curry dishes. Once you have discovered how quick and easy they are to prepare, you will want to cook them again and again.

Serve them with rice (see page 48 for saffron rice), chappati (page 55) or naan (page 47). They are also delicious with either a simple side salad of crispy lettuce, onion and tomato wedges. Or try some steamed vegetables to which you can add some chopped tomato flesh or some finely chopped fresh chilli, if you wish.

CHICKEN TIKKA MASALA

POINTS

per recipe: $7\frac{1}{2}$ per serving: $3\frac{1}{2}$

Serves 2
Preparation and cooking time: 45
minutes + 20 minutes – 10 hours
marinating
Calories per serving: 255
Freezing: not recommended

Serve with a salad of iceberg lettuce, sliced onions and tomato wedges and either 4 tablespoons of cooked plain basmati rice (3 points) or a naan (see page 47; 4 points).

2 small chicken breasts, each weighing
150 g (5½ oz) and each cut into 8 or
10 pieces
a few sprigs of fresh coriander, to
garnish (optional)

FOR THE MARINADE
2 tablespoons low-fat plain bio yogurt
1 tablespoon tandoori spice powder
1 tablespoon lemon juice

FOR THE MASALA SAUCE
low-fat cooking spray
1 medium onion, chopped
2 garlic cloves, crushed
2.5 cm (1-inch) piece of fresh root
ginger, grated
1 teaspoon medium-strength curry
powder
½ teaspoon mild chilli powder
½ teaspoon cumin seeds
1 tablespoon tomato purée
15 g (½ oz) ground almonds
1 tablespoon lemon juice
1 tablespoon half-fat crème fraîche

1 Mix together the marinade ingredients. Put the chicken pieces in a dish, pour the marinade over and stir well to mix. Cover the dish and put in the fridge to marinate for at least 20 minutes, but preferably 8–10 hours.

2 When ready to cook, preheat the grill or griddle.

3 Heat a non-stick pan and spray with the low-fat cooking spray. Stir-fry the onion for about 8 minutes until soft and brown.

4 Add all the sauce ingredients to the pan, except the crème fraîche, together with 100 ml (3½ fl oz) water. Heat gently until simmering, then cover the pan with a tight-fitting lid and cook gently for 15 minutes.

5 Grill or griddle the chicken pieces for about 12–15 minutes, turning to cook on all sides until just starting to blacken and the chicken is cooked through.

6 Remove the lid from the pan and heat for a few minutes until the sauce has reduced and thickened slightly. Stir in the crème fraîche then add the chicken pieces. Simmer gently for 15 minutes more before serving. If desired, garnish with fresh coriander.

TOP TIP Tandoori spice powder is easy to make yourself. Simply mix together 1 teaspoon each of medium-strength curry powder, turmeric and chilli powder.

CHICKEN MASSALAM

POINTS

per recipe: 11   per serving: 3

Serves 4
Preparation time: 10 minutes + 30
minutes soaking
Cooking time: 1 hour
Calories per serving: 185
Freezing: not recommended

Massalam is another form of the word 'masala' which refers to any combination of spices used in an Indian dish (see general introduction). The saffron turns the chicken a lovely yellow colour. Serve it with tomato and coriander salad (page 55).

4 small chicken breasts, weighing
150 g (5½ oz) each
a pinch of saffron threads, soaked in
2 tablespoons hot water for at least
30 minutes, soaking liquid reserved

salt and freshly ground black pepper
a handful of coriander leaves, to
garnish

FOR THE SAUCE

juice of 1 lemon
5 cm (2-inch) piece of fresh root ginger,
grated
1 garlic clove, crushed
½ cinnamon stick
6 cardamom pods, crushed slightly
1 teaspoon turmeric
½ teaspoon salt
½ teaspoon cumin seeds
150 ml (5 fl oz) low-fat plain bio yogurt

1 Preheat the oven to Gas Mark 4/180°C/350°F.
2 Place the chicken breasts in a single layer in a flameproof, ovenproof dish.
3 Mix the saffron and its soaking water with the other sauce ingredients and pour over the chicken. Cover with a tight-fitting lid and bake for 55 minutes.

4 Remove the chicken from the dish and set to one side keeping it warm while preparing the sauce.
5 Pour the cooking juices from the dish into a food processor or liquidiser and whizz until smooth. Return to the dish and warm through on the hob for a few minutes until the sauce has reduced and thickened slightly.
6 Divide the sauce between four serving plates, place a chicken breast in the middle of each. Season to taste and serve garnished with a few coriander leaves.

TOP TIP If you do not have a flameproof, ovenproof dish, at step 5, liquidise the juices then pour into a small saucepan to reheat.

CUMIN-SPICED CHICKEN

POINTS

per recipe: 2½   per serving: 2½

Serves 1
Preparation and cooking time: 25
minutes
Calories per serving: 220
Freezing: not recommended

Cumin is a very ancient spice, originally from Syria and Egypt. This recipe demonstrates a very popular way of cooking chicken in India. Serve with steamed broccoli and garnish with some chopped red chilli for no extra points.

low-fat cooking spray
½ large onion, sliced
1 skinless and boned chicken breast,
weighing 150 g (5½ oz), cut into
8 pieces
1 garlic clove, crushed
½ teaspoon cumin seeds
½ teaspoon ground coriander
½ teaspoon ground cumin
¼ teaspoon salt
¼ teaspoon turmeric
1 medium green chilli, de-seeded and
chopped
150 ml (5 fl oz) chicken stock
1 tablespoon lemon juice
1 tablespoon 0% fat Greek-style
natural yogurt
salt and freshly ground black pepper

1 Heat a non-stick frying pan and spray with the low-fat cooking spray. Stir-fry the onion for about 4 minutes until soft.
2 Add the chicken pieces to the pan and continue to cook for 2–3 minutes until they are brown on all sides.
3 Add all the other ingredients, except the lemon juice and yogurt. Heat gently until simmering, then cover the pan with a tight-fitting lid and cook for 15 minutes.
4 Remove the lid and cook for 2–3 more minutes until the sauce has reduced and thickened.
5 Stir in the lemon juice and yogurt, season to taste then serve.

CHICKEN PILAU

POINTS

per recipe: 5   per serving: 5

Serves 1
Preparation and cooking time: 40 minutes
Calories per serving: 390
Freezing: not recommended

---

low-fat cooking spray

1 small chicken breast, weighing 150 g (5^1/$_2$ oz), cut into 3 pieces

50 g (1^3/$_4$ oz) basmati rice

1 garlic clove, crushed

^{1}/$_2$ teaspoon chilli powder

^{1}/$_2$ teaspoon cumin seeds

^{1}/$_2$ teaspoon turmeric

2.5 cm (1-inch) cinnamon stick

2 cardamom pods, crushed slightly

1 tablespoon lemon juice

1 tablespoon low-fat plain bio yogurt

200 ml (7 fl oz) chicken stock

^{1}/$_2$ medium onion, sliced

salt and freshly ground black pepper

---

1 Heat a non-stick frying pan and spray with the low-fat cooking spray. Stir-fry the chicken for 2–3 minutes until brown on all sides.

2 Add all the other ingredients, except the onion, to the pan. Heat gently until simmering, then cover the pan with a tight-fitting lid and cook for 12–15 minutes until most of the stock has been absorbed and the rice is cooked.

3 Meanwhile, heat another non-stick pan and spray with cooking spray. Stir-fry the onion for about 10 minutes until soft and brown.

4 When the pilau is cooked, drain it, put into a serving bowl and cover with a clean, dry tea towel. Set it aside for 2 minutes.

5 Season the rice to taste and stir in the onion.

CORIANDER CHICKEN

POINTS

per recipe: 5^1/$_2$ per serving: 3

Serves 2
Preparation time: 15 minutes
Cooking time: 15 minutes
Calories per serving: 190
Freezing: not recommended

---

low-fat cooking spray

2 skinless chicken breasts, weighing 150 g (5^1/$_2$ oz) each, cubed

2 garlic cloves, crushed

2.5 cm (1-inch) piece of fresh root ginger, grated

1 teaspoon ground coriander

^{1}/$_2$ teaspoon ground cumin

^{1}/$_2$ teaspoon turmeric

50 ml (2 fl oz) low-fat plain bio yogurt

1 tablespoon lemon juice

2 tablespoons chopped fresh coriander leaves

---

1 Heat a non-stick frying pan and spray with the low-fat cooking spray. Stir-fry the chicken for about 2–3 minutes, until brown on all sides.

2 Add the garlic, ginger and spices. Make the yogurt up to 100 ml (3^1/$_2$ fl oz) with water and add to the pan together with the lemon juice.

3 Heat gently until simmering, then cover the pan with a tight-fitting lid and cook for 15 minutes.

4 When the chicken is cooked, stir in the coriander leaves.

Chicken pilau: This is similar to a Spanish paella but it has a distinctly Indian flavour.

CHICKEN BALTI

POINTS

per recipe: **5½**   per serving: **3**

Serves 2
Preparation time: 15 minutes
Cooking time: 20 minutes
Calories per serving: 225
Freezing: not recommended

Although the balti originally came from Pakistan, it has been enthusiastically adopted by Indian restaurants in Britain. Its appeal comes from the variety of ingredients that can be used. Serve with naan bread (page 47) for 4 extra points.

low-fat cooking spray
1 medium onion, sliced
1 medium red pepper, de-seeded and cut into thick strips

2 chicken breasts, weighing 150 g (5½ oz) each, diced
1 garlic clove, crushed
2.5 cm (1-inch) piece of fresh root ginger, grated
1 medium green chilli, de-seeded and chopped finely
1 teaspoon medium-strength curry powder
2 cardamom pods, crushed slightly
½ teaspoon cumin seeds
3 tablespoons low-fat plain bio yogurt
1 tablespoon lemon juice
salt and freshly ground black pepper
fresh coriander leaves, to garnish

1 Heat a non-stick pan and spray with the low-fat cooking spray. Stir-fry the onion and pepper for about 5 minutes until soft.

2 Add the chicken to the pan and cook for 2–3 minutes or until brown on all sides.

3 Add all the other ingredients to the pan. Heat gently until simmering, then cover the pan with a tight-fitting lid and cook for 15 minutes.

4 Remove the lid, and heat for a few minutes more until the sauce has reduced and thickened slightly.

5 Season to taste then serve, garnished with coriander leaves.

VARIATION Make a vegetable balti by substituting the chicken with 250 g (9 oz) mushrooms and 2 large handfuls of chopped fresh spinach. Add the spinach at step 4 when you remove the lid and cook until the spinach has wilted. This will be 0 points per serving.

CHICKEN KORMA

POINTS

per recipe: **5**   per serving: **5**

Serves 1
Preparation and cooking time: 30 minutes
Calories per serving: 350
Freezing: not recommended

Korma refers to a cooking method, not a taste. Usually the liquid is added towards the end of the cooking time and is allowed to evaporate off or 'reduce' before the dish is served. This is a mild, creamy curry which is good served with steamed green beans, mixed with a little chopped tomato flesh and an Indian bread, such as naan (page 47, 4 points per serving) to mop up the sauce.

low-fat cooking spray
1 medium onion, sliced thinly
1 chicken breast, weighing 150 g (5½ oz), cubed
1 garlic clove, crushed
2.5 cm (1-inch) piece of fresh root ginger, grated
½ cinnamon stick
2 cardamom pods, crushed slightly
½ teaspoon cumin seeds
½ teaspoon mild chilli powder
½ teaspoon turmeric
50 ml (2 fl oz) 0% fat Greek-style natural yogurt
100 ml (3½ fl oz) low-fat plain bio yogurt
1 tablespoon ground almonds
3 tablespoons skimmed milk
salt and freshly ground black pepper
a few sprigs of fresh coriander, to garnish (optional)

1 Heat a non-stick pan and spray with the low-fat cooking spray. Stir-fry the onion for about 5 minutes until soft.

2 Add the chicken pieces to the pan and cook for 5 minutes or until brown on all sides.

3 Add the rest of the ingredients, except the skimmed milk. Heat gently until simmering, then cover the pan with a tight-fitting lid and cook for 15 minutes.

4 Remove the lid and cook for a few minutes more to concentrate the flavour of the sauce, then add the skimmed milk and stir well to mix.

5 Season to taste, garnish with coriander, if using, and serve.

Chicken korma: Kormas are deservedly one of our favourite curries; they have a deliciously exotic creaminess.

Pork jalfrezi:
Pork is so tasty
cooked with
peppers, ginger
and Indian spices.

PORK JALFREZI

POINTS

per recipe: 7   per serving: 2

Serves 4
Preparation and cooking time: 30
minutes
Calories per serving: 185
Freezing: recommended

Jalfrezi dishes are spicy, stir-fried curries. They are also cooked quickly so the meat needs to be cut into small pieces in order for it to cook properly. Serve with fresh mango chutney (page 51) and add on 1 extra point per serving.

low-fat cooking spray
2 medium onions, chopped
2 medium red peppers, de-seeded and chopped
1 tablespoon tomato purée
300 g (10½ oz) pork escalopes, cubed

1 green pepper, de-seeded and sliced thinly
2 garlic cloves, crushed
5 cm (2-inch) piece of fresh root ginger, grated
1 medium green chilli, de-seeded and chopped finely
1 tablespoon medium-strength curry powder
1 teaspoon chilli powder
1 teaspoon cumin seeds
500 g (1 lb 2 oz) passata (sieved tomatoes)
1 tablespoon chopped fresh coriander leaves
salt and freshly ground black pepper

1 Heat a non-stick pan and spray with the low-fat cooking spray. Stir-fry the onions and red peppers for about 8 minutes until the peppers are soft and the onion is brown.
2 Put the onion and red pepper mixture into a food processor or liquidiser. Add the tomato purée and whizz until smooth. Set aside.
3 Heat the non-stick pan and spray again with the low-fat cooking spray. Stir-fry the pork and green peppers for 5–10 minutes until brown.
4 Return the onion and pepper purée to the pan then add all other ingredients, except the seasoning and coriander. Heat gently until simmering, then cover the pan with a tight-fitting lid and cook for 10 minutes.
5 Remove the lid and cook for 2–3 minutes more until the sauce is reduced and thickened slightly.
6 Season to taste then stir in the coriander leaves and serve.

VARIATION Substitute the pork with 3 chicken breasts weighing 150 g (5½ oz) each, cut into bite-size pieces. Cook for 15 minutes instead of 10 minutes at Step 4. The points will remain the same.

TURKEY MADRAS

POINTS

per recipe: 4½   per serving: 2½

Serves 2
Preparation and cooking time: 10
minutes
Cooking time: 20 minutes
Calories per serving: 215
Freezing: recommended

Another British invention, Madras tends to be synonymous with hot! Although this version is not too hot, it is lovely served with the cooling cucumber raita (page 51) for an extra ½ point.

low-fat cooking spray
1 medium onion, chopped
300 g (10½ oz) turkey breast, diced
1 garlic clove
2.5 cm (1-inch) piece of fresh root ginger, grated
1 medium green chilli, de-seeded and chopped finely
1 tablespoon medium-strength curry powder
2 cardamom pods, crushed slightly
2 teaspoons chilli powder
1 teaspoon ground coriander
½ teaspoon cumin seeds
200 ml (7 fl oz) chicken stock
salt and freshly ground black pepper

1 Heat a non-stick pan and spray with the low-fat cooking spray. Stir-fry the onion for about 5 minutes until soft.
2 Add the turkey to the pan and cook for 2–3 minutes or until brown on all sides.
3 Add the remaining ingredients. Heat gently until simmering, then cover the pan with a tight-fitting lid and cook for 15 minutes.
4 Remove the lid and cook for 2–3 minutes more until the sauce has reduced and thickened slightly.
5 Season to taste then serve.

VARIATION Make this with chicken instead of turkey. The points will remain the same.

LAMB CHOPS IN MASALA SAUCE

POINTS

per recipe: 14	per serving: 3½

Serves 4
Preparation and cooking time: 25 minutes
Calories per serving: 300
Freezing: not recommended

A very tasty way of serving lamb chops. Serve with a salad of iceberg lettuce, onion rings and tomatoes. Oven-baked chilli chips (page 52) go with this, but don't forget to add on 3 extra points.

4 lamb chops, weighing 125 g (4½ oz) each, trimmed of all fat
2 garlic cloves, halved
a pinch of chilli powder
low-fat cooking spray
salt and freshly ground black pepper

FOR THE SAUCE

200 ml (7 fl oz) low-fat plain bio yogurt
juice of 1 lemon
1 medium red chilli, de-seeded and chopped finely
5 cm (2-inch) piece of fresh root ginger, grated
2 garlic cloves, crushed
2 teaspoons ground cumin
2 teaspoons ground coriander
1 teaspoon turmeric
1 teaspoon chilli powder
2 tablespoons tomato purée
100 ml (3½ fl oz) passata (sieved tomatoes)

1 Preheat the griddle or grill to a medium heat.
2 Season the chops by rubbing with the halves of garlic and sprinkling with chilli powder and black pepper.
3 Spray the chops lightly with the low-fat cooking spray then griddle or grill them for about 6–8 minutes on each side.
4 Mix together the sauce ingredients in a small pan and heat gently for 2–3 minutes prior to serving.
5 To serve, divide the sauce between the serving plates then place a lamb chop in the middle of each.

TOP TIP Used sieved rather than canned tomatoes in this recipe as they give a smoother, creamier sauce.

VARIATIONS Substitute fresh chopped tomatoes if you prefer a chunkier sauce.

Substitute the lamb chops with lamb leg steaks, each weighing 100 g (3½ oz) which will be 3 points per serving.

LAMB ROGAN JOSH

POINTS

per recipe: 32	per serving: 8

Serves 4
Preparation time: 20 minutes
Cooking time: 45 minutes
Calories per serving: 255
Freezing: recommended

A rogan josh is very aromatic since the meat is cooked very slowly, allowing all the flavours to develop. It goes very well with spinach garnished with chopped red chilli.

low-fat cooking spray
3 medium onions, sliced
400 g (14 oz) lamb neck fillet, diced
2 garlic cloves, crushed
2.5 cm (1-inch) piece of fresh root ginger, grated
1 cinnamon stick
2 cardamom pods, crushed slightly
2 teaspoons ground coriander
1 teaspoon chilli powder
½ teaspoon cumin seeds
½ teaspoon turmeric
2 tablespoons tomato purée
400 g can of chopped tomatoes
salt and freshly ground black pepper

1 Preheat the oven to Gas Mark 4/ 180°C/350°F.
2 Heat a non-stick flameproof, ovenproof dish and spray with the low-fat cooking spray. Stir-fry the onions for about 8 minutes until soft and brown.
3 Add the diced lamb to the dish and stir-fry for about 2–3 minutes until brown on all sides.
4 Add the remaining ingredients. Heat gently until simmering, then cover the pan with a tight-fitting lid and cook for 45 minutes.
5 Remove from the oven, season to taste and serve.

TOP TIP Do not allow the curry to boil at step 4 otherwise the meat may become tough.

Lamb chops in masala sauce: Enjoy these spicy chops with chips for a total of only 6½ points.

**Lamb saag:
Spinach lends
a fresh taste to
this dish and
it's good for
you too!**

LAMB SAAG

Serves 4
Preparation and cooking time: 25
minutes
Calories per serving: 285
Freezing: recommended

Saag is a medium-strength curry
cooked with spinach.

low-fat cooking spray
2 medium onions, chopped
400 g (14 oz) lean lamb neck fillet,
diced
2 garlic cloves, crushed
5 cm (2-inch) piece of fresh root
ginger, grated
1 medium green chilli, de-seeded and
chopped finely
1 tablespoon medium-strength curry
powder
1 teaspoon chilli powder
1 teaspoon ground coriander
2 × 400 g can of chopped tomatoes
225 g (8 oz) baby spinach
salt and freshly ground black pepper

1 Heat a non-stick pan and spray
with the low-fat cooking spray. Stir-
fry the onions for about 5 minutes
until soft.
2 Add the diced lamb to the pan and
cook for 2–3 minutes until brown on
all sides.
3 Add all other ingredients to the
pan, except the spinach. Heat gently
until simmering, then cover the pan
with a tight-fitting lid and cook for
5 minutes.
4 Remove the lid, add the spinach
and continue to cook for about 2–3
minutes or until the spinach has
wilted into the curry and the sauce
has reduced and thickened slightly.
5 Season to taste then serve.

LAMB BHUNA

Serves 4
Preparation and cooking time: 20
minutes
Calories per serving: 265
Freezing: recommended

The term 'bhuna' is used when spices
are cooked in hot oil. This low-point
version has a creamy-tasting, thick
sauce that clings to the meat. Serve
it with steamed cauliflower and a
pinch of poppy seeds.

low-fat cooking spray
2 medium onions, chopped
400 g (14 oz) lean lamb, e.g. neck
fillet, diced finely
2 garlic cloves, crushed
5 cm (2-inch) piece of fresh root
ginger, grated
1½ tablespoons medium-strength
curry powder
2 teaspoons turmeric
4 tablespoons tomato purée
2 tablespoons tamarind paste
salt and freshly ground black pepper

1 Heat a non-stick frying pan and
spray with the low-fat cooking
spray. Stir-fry the onions for about
8 minutes until soft and brown.
2 Add the lamb to the frying pan
and stir-fry until the lamb is browned
on all sides.
3 Add the rest of the ingredients
together with 150 ml (¼ pint) water.
Stir well, and heat gently until
simmering, then cover the pan
with a tight-fitting lid and cook for
5 minutes. Do not allow it to boil as
this will cause the meat to become
tough.
4 Remove the lid, season to taste,
stir well then serve.

CORIANDER MINCED BEEF

Serves 4
Preparation and cooking time: 30
minutes
Calories per serving: 175
Freezing: not recommended

low-fat cooking spray
2 medium onions, sliced thinly
250 g (9 oz) extra-lean minced beef
2 garlic cloves, crushed
5 cm (2-inch) piece of fresh root
ginger, grated
2 medium green chillies, de-seeded
and chopped finely
1 medium red chilli, de-seeded and
chopped finely
1 tablespoon medium-strength curry
powder
2 cardamom pods, crushed slightly
1 teaspoon ground coriander
1 teaspoon ground cumin
2 tablespoons tomato purée
400 g can of chopped tomatoes
4 tablespoons frozen peas
2 tablespoons chopped fresh
coriander leaves
salt and freshly ground black pepper

1 Heat a non-stick pan and spray
with cooking spray. Stir-fry the
onions for 8 minutes or until soft
and brown.
2 Add the meat and fry for 2–3
minutes until brown.
3 Add all the other ingredients, except
the peas and coriander leaves.
Heat gently until simmering, then
cover the pan with a tight-fitting
lid and cook for 10 minutes.
4 Stir the peas into the mixture, cover
again and cook for 5 minutes more.
5 Season to taste, stir in the coriander
leaves and serve.

King prawn saag:
A meal of spicy,
aromatic prawns
for only 1½ points
per serving.

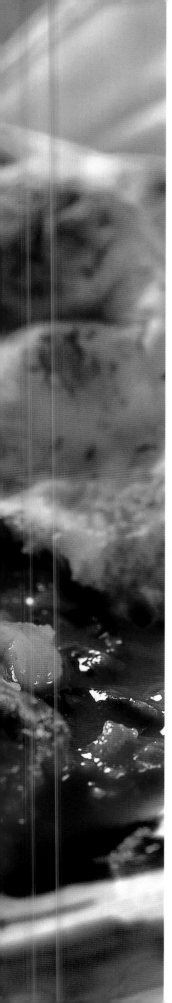

fish
curries

Being a low-calorie, low-fat food, most of us should be eating more fish than we currently do. It is a great alternative to meat dishes and I hope that these great fish curries will encourage you to eat more fish.

Oven-baked chilli chips (page 52) go particularly well with a fish curry but 4 tablespoons of plain boiled rice (3 points), naan bread (page 47), or chappati (page 55) would also be good accompaniments.

KING PRAWN SAAG

POINTS	
per recipe: 3	per serving: 1½

Serves 2
Preparation and cooking time: 25 minutes
Calories per serving: 160
Freezing: not recommended

This is another quick-and-easy curry, which uses prawns and is delicious served with plain basmati rice (3 points for 4 tablespoons) and Roasted Tomato and Chilli Chutney (page 51).

low-fat cooking spray

1 medium onion, chopped

1 garlic clove, crushed

2.5 cm (1-inch) piece of fresh root ginger, grated

½ tablespoon medium-strength curry powder

1 teaspoon ground coriander

½ teaspoon chilli powder

400 g can of chopped tomatoes

200 g (7 oz) raw king prawns, heads and shells removed, de-frosted if frozen and patted dry on kitchen paper

100 g (3½ oz) baby spinach

salt and freshly ground black pepper

1 Heat a non-stick pan and spray with the low-fat cooking spray. Stir-fry the onion for about 5 minutes until soft.

2 Add all the ingredients to the pan, except the prawns and spinach, and heat gently until simmering, then cover the pan with a tight-fitting lid and cook for 10 minutes.

3 Remove the lid, add the prawns and spinach and stir-fry for 4–5 minutes or until the prawns are bright pink and the spinach has wilted.

4 Season to taste and serve.

Fish korma: The ideal tasty after-work supper – it's ready in only 15 minutes.

FISH KORMA

POINTS

per recipe: 3	per serving: 3

Serves 1
Preparation and cooking time: 15 minutes
Calories per serving: 250
Freezing: not recommended

Cardamoms come in three different colours, each with a slightly different flavour. In a traditional korma, brown cardamoms are used, which give a slightly astringent flavour. Serve it with spinach garnished with some skinned, chopped tomato (see page 17 for a tip on skinning tomatoes).

low-fat cooking spray
1/2 medium onion, chopped
1 haddock fish fillet, weighing 200 g (7 oz), cubed
1 garlic clove, crushed
2.5 cm (1-inch) piece of fresh root ginger, grated
100 ml (3 1/2 fl oz) low-fat plain bio yogurt
2.5 cm (1-inch) cinnamon stick
1 cardamom pod, crushed slightly
1/2 teaspoon turmeric
1/4 teaspoon cumin seeds
1/4 teaspoon chilli powder
salt and freshly ground black pepper
1 medium green chilli cut into rings, to garnish (optional)

1 Heat a non-stick pan and spray with the low-fat cooking spray. Fry the onion for about 5 minutes until soft.

2 Add the rest of the ingredients to the pan, stir and heat gently until simmering, then cover the pan with a tight-fitting lid and cook for 6–7 minutes until the fish is cooked through.

3 Season to taste and garnish with rings of fresh green chilli, if using.

VARIATION Make a prawn korma by substituting the fish with 100 g (3 1/2 oz) cooked large tiger prawns. Make the curry sauce first and then stir in the prawns and heat through before serving. This will be 2 points per serving.

FISH FILLETS WITH CURRY SAUCE

POINTS

per recipe: 7	per serving: 3 1/2

Serves 2
Preparation and cooking time: 25 minutes + 30 minutes soaking
Calories per serving: 245
Freezing: not recommended

This is more of a colonial Indian dish than a traditional one. Serve with steamed green beans for no extra points.

2 small white fish fillets e.g cod or haddock, weighing 200 g (7 oz) each
a small a pinch of saffron strands soaked for at least 30 minutes in 2 tablespoons warm skimmed milk, reserving the soaking liquid
a small pinch of chilli powder
salt and freshly ground black pepper

FOR THE CURRY SAUCE
150 ml (1/4 pint) skimmed milk
15 g (1/2 oz) half-fat butter
15 g (1/2 oz) plain white flour
1 teaspoon curry powder
1/2 teaspoon turmeric

1 Preheat the oven to Gas Mark 6/ 200°C/400°F.

2 Place the fish on a piece of cooking foil on a baking sheet. Pour the saffron and its soaking liquid over the fish and season with a little chilli powder, salt and freshly ground black pepper. Wrap the foil loosely around the fish to make a parcel and bake for 20 minutes.

3 After 15 minutes make the sauce by mixing all the sauce ingredients in a small non-stick pan. Heat gently until simmering, then cook for 2–3 minutes, stirring frequently.

4 Serve the fish fillets out of the parcels with the sauce poured over.

Fish fillets with curry sauce: The delicious taste of fish with saffron and spices is well worth the effort!

MIXED SEAFOOD CURRY

POINTS	
per recipe: 10	per serving: 2½

Serves 4
Preparation & cooking time: 25 minutes
Calories per serving: 185
Freezing: not recommended

This comes from the eastern Bengali state and is delicious with cucumber chutney, (page 48) and plain basmati rice (4 tablespoons are 3 points).

low-fat cooking spray

2 onions, chopped finely

2 garlic cloves, crushed

5 cm (2-inch) piece of grated fresh root ginger, grated

350 g (12 oz) skinned cod fillet, cut into bite-sized pieces

150 ml (5 fl oz) 0% Greek-style natural yogurt

150 ml (5 fl oz) low-fat plain bio yogurt

1 tablespoon medium-strength curry powder

1 teaspoon turmeric

1 red chilli, de-seeded and chopped finely

250 g (9 oz) mixed seafood selection, drained and dried on kitchen paper

salt and freshly ground black pepper

1 Heat a non-stick saucepan, spray with the low-fat cooking spray and cook the onions until soft but still uncoloured – about 4 minutes.
2 Add all ingredients except the mixed seafood selection. Bring up to a gentle heat, cover and cook for 5 minutes. Uncover and add the seafood. Continue to cook until the seafood has been heated through and the fish is completely cooked. Do not overcook or the seafood will toughen.
3 Season and serve.

Prawn masala: So easy and scrumptious.

PRAWN MASALA

POINTS	
per recipe: 5½	per serving: 3

Serves 2
Preparation and cooking time: 20 minutes
Calories per serving: 230
Freezing: not recommended

low-fat cooking spray

2 medium onions, chopped

1 medium red pepper, de-seeded and diced

200 ml (7 fl oz) passata (sieved tomatoes)

100 ml (3½ fl oz) low-fat plain bio yogurt

1 tablespoon lemon juice

2 tablespoons tomato purée

2 teaspoons curry powder

½ teaspoon chilli powder

½ teaspoon cumin seeds

200 g (7 oz) cooked prawns, defrosted

1 Heat a non-stick pan and spray with the low-fat cooking spray. Stir-fry the onions and pepper for about 5 minutes until the pepper is starting to soften and the onion is turning brown.
2 Add all the other ingredients except the prawns. Heat gently to a simmer. Cover the pan with a tight-fitting lid and cook for 5 minutes.
3 Remove the lid and cook for a few minutes more until the sauce has reduced and thickened slightly.
4 Stir in the prawns. Heat through.

TUNA BALTI

POINTS

per recipe: $2\frac{1}{2}$ per serving: $1\frac{1}{2}$

Serves 2

Preparation and cooking time: 25 minutes

Calories per serving: 210

Freezing: not recommended

low-fat cooking spray

2 medium onions, sliced

300 g ($10\frac{1}{2}$ oz) mixed zero point vegetables, sliced thinly e.g. red and green peppers, courgettes and mushrooms

2 garlic cloves, crushed

5 cm (2-inch) piece of fresh root ginger, grated

1 medium green chilli, de-seeded and chopped finely

2 tablespoons 0% fat Greek-style natural yogurt

1 tablespoon tomato purée

$\frac{1}{2}$ tablespoon medium-strength curry powder

200 g can of tuna steak in brine or spring water, drained and broken into large chunks

1 tablespoon chopped fresh coriander leaves

1 tablespoon half-fat crème fraîche

salt and freshly ground black pepper

1 Heat a non-stick pan. Spray with the cooking spray. Stir-fry the onions for 5 minutes until soft.

2 Add the vegetables. Stir-fry for 4–5 minutes until cooked through.

3 Stir in the garlic, ginger, chilli, yogurt, tomato purée and curry powder together with 3 tablespoons water. Heat gently until simmering, then cover the pan with a tight-fitting lid and cook for 5 minutes more.

4 Remove the lid, add the tuna steak, coriander and crème fraîche to the pan, stirring gently to mix. Season.

KING PRAWN VINDALOO

POINTS

per recipe: $1\frac{1}{2}$ per serving: $1\frac{1}{2}$

Serves 1

Preparation and cooking time: 25 minutes

Calories per serving: 155

Freezing: not recommended

low-fat cooking spray

1 medium onion, chopped

1 garlic clove, crushed

2.5 cm (1-inch) piece of fresh root ginger, grated

1 tablespoon white wine vinegar

$\frac{1}{2}$ tablespoon medium-strength curry powder

1 teaspoon chilli powder

$\frac{1}{2}$ teaspoon sugar

100 g ($3\frac{1}{2}$ oz) raw king prawns, heads and shells removed, de-frosted

1 Heat a non-stick pan and spray with the low-fat cooking spray. Stir-fry the onion for about 8 minutes until soft and brown.

2 In a bowl mix together all other ingredients, except for the king prawns, with 4 tablespoons water.

3 Add this mixture to the pan with the onion and mix well. Add the prawns. Heat gently until simmering, then cover the pan with a tight-fitting lid and cook for 4–5 minutes, or until the prawns have turned bright pink.

Tuna balti:
A fantastic curry for only $1\frac{1}{2}$ points per serving.

CREAMY SALMON CURRY

POINTS

per recipe: 6½   per serving: 6½

Serves 1
Preparation and cooking time: 20 minutes
Calories per serving: 375
Freezing: not recommended

This recipe is based on a Kashmiri curry, which is mild and creamy. Serve with steamed broccoli tossed with Bombay-style Potatoes (page 52) for 2 extra points.

1 salmon fillet, weighing 125 g (4½ oz)

a pinch of chilli powder

salt and freshly ground black pepper

FOR THE SAUCE

150 ml (¼ pint) low-fat plain bio yogurt

1 garlic clove, crushed

2.5 cm (1-inch) piece of fresh root ginger, grated

1 medium red chilli, chopped finely

15 g (½ oz) ground almonds

½ teaspoon medium-strength curry powder

½ teaspoon turmeric

½ tablespoon chopped fresh coriander leaves

1 Preheat the grill to a medium to high heat.

2 Season the salmon fillet with chilli powder, salt and black pepper. Cook, skin-side down for 4–6 minutes. Turn and cook for another 4–6 minutes.

3 Meanwhile, put all the sauce ingredients except the coriander into a small pan and heat gently until simmering, stirring frequently. Cover and cook for 5 minutes more.

4 Stir the chopped coriander into the sauce, season to taste and pour the sauce on to a serving plate. Place the salmon fillet in the middle of the sauce, skin-side up and serve.

FISH MADRAS

POINTS

per recipe: 5   per serving: 2½

Serves 2
Preparation and cooking time: 25 minutes
Calories per serving: 240
Freezing: not recommended

This curry is quite hot so serve with cucumber or mint raita (page 51) to cool you down, adding an extra ½ point per serving.

2 small cod fillets, each weighing 200 g (7 oz), cut into 4 pieces

a sprinkling of chilli powder

salt and freshly ground black pepper

FOR THE SAUCE

low-fat cooking spray

1 medium onion, chopped

2 garlic cloves, crushed

5 cm (2-inch) piece of fresh root ginger, grated

1 medium green chilli, de-seeded and chopped finely

2 tablespoons medium-strength curry powder

2 teaspoons chilli powder

1 teaspoon ground coriander

½ teaspoon cumin seeds

200 ml (7 fl oz) fish stock

1 Preheat the grill or griddle.

2 Season the fish with a sprinkling of chilli powder, salt and pepper.

3 Cook under the grill for 10–15 minutes depending on the thickness of the fillet, turning once during cooking. To check the fish is cooked through, lift the skin with the point of a sharp knife. If the flesh has turned white it is ready.

4 Meanwhile, heat a non-stick pan and spray with the low-fat cooking spray. Stir-fry the onion for about 5 minutes until soft.

5 Add the rest of the sauce ingredients to the pan and heat gently until simmering, then cover the pan with a tight-fitting lid and cook for 5 minutes more.

6 Remove the skin from the fish and discard. Gently mix the flesh with the sauce and serve immediately.

Creamy salmon curry: Almonds, curry and ginger complement the rich flavour of salmon so well.

Naan bread:
Delicious and
easy to make –
only 4 points
each!

side dishes

There are many accompaniments that you can serve with your Indian meal. Sometimes you may just want to serve plain rice (4 tablespoons are 3 points), but at others times you may want to serve something a little different such as saffron rice (page 48) or an Indian bread such as chappati (page 55) or naan. Potatoes can be also cooked in many different ways and make a delicious alternative to rice.

You could serve a plain salad with curry, but you could also accompany it with a cooling raita if it is a particularly hot curry. To add freshness, serve a curry with Tomato and Coriander Salad (page 55) or Fresh Mango Chutney (page 51).

NAAN BREAD

POINTS

per recipe: **23**   per serving: **4**

 Makes 6

Preparation time: 30 minutes + 24 hours chilling + 15 minutes rising
Cooking time: 5–10 minutes
Calories per serving: 265
Freezing: recommended

Naan bread is traditionally served with balti dishes but is good with any Indian food.

425 g (15 oz) plain white flour plus extra for sprinkling

1 teaspoon salt

150 ml (5 fl oz) low-fat plain bio yogurt

1 teaspoon active dried yeast

low-fat cooking spray

½ tablespoon poppy seeds, for sprinkling

1 Place the flour, salt, yogurt and yeast in a bowl and use up to 150 ml (¼ pint) warm water to form a dough.
2 Knead for 5 minutes until the dough is soft and feels springy.
3 Cover with clingfilm and chill in the fridge for at least 4–5 hours or, preferably, overnight.
4 Uncover the dough and knead for 3 minutes, then cover again and chill for at least 4–5 hours.
5 Divide the dough into 6 equal pieces and roll each into a ball. Flatten into an oval and gently pull into a longer oval so that the dough is about the thickness of your fingers.
6 Preheat the oven to its highest temperature.
7 Lightly spray two baking sheets with the low-fat cooking spray then sprinkle with flour. Place the naan breads on the prepared sheets and leave to rest for 15 minutes.

8 Sprinkle the naan breads with a little water and a small sprinkling of poppy seeds and then bake for 5–10 minutes or until the surface of the naans bubble up and start to brown.
9 Serve immediately or cool and freeze until needed.

TOP TIPS The time these naan breads take to cook will depend on how hot your oven is and how thick or thin that you have made them.

Naans wrapped well in plastic wrap will keep in the fridge for one day.

To freeze, wrap each one well in plastic wrap. Store in the freezer for up to 1 month.

CUCUMBER CHUTNEY

POINTS

per recipe: ½   per serving: 0

 ⓥ Ⓥɢ *Serves 4*

Preparation time: 10 minutes + 20
minutes chilling
Calories per serving: 15
Freezing: not recommended

Tiny poppy seeds are used to provide flavour and decoration in Indian dishes. The flavour is mild and slightly nutty. Here they are used in a very spicy but refreshing side dish.

½ medium cucumber, sliced very
thinly into long strips
1 garlic clove, crushed
1 medium green chilli, de-seeded and
chopped finely
1 tablespoon white wine vinegar
1 teaspoon sugar
a pinch of poppy seeds

1 Put the cucumber into a sieve and press as much liquid out of the strips as you can with the back of a wooden spoon.
2 Chop the cucumber then place in a serving bowl.
3 Mix together the garlic, chilli, vinegar and sugar and stir until the sugar has dissolved.
4 Pour this mixture over the cucumber then sprinkle with poppy seeds and chill for at least 20 minutes before serving.

SAFFRON RICE

POINTS

per recipe: 12½   per serving: 3

ⓥ Ⓥɢ *Serves 4*

Preparation and cooking time: 20
minutes + at least 30 minutes soaking
Calories per serving: 225
Freezing: not recommended

An aromatic rice dish to serve with your curries.

250 g (9 oz) basmati rice, rinsed under
cold running water and drained
a pinch of saffron strands, soaked in
a little boiling water for at least
30 minutes, then drained
juice of ½ lemon
½ teaspoon cumin seeds
4 cardamom pods, crushed slightly
2.5 cm (1-inch) piece of cinnamon stick
salt and freshly ground black pepper

1 Place all the ingredients in a pan and cover with cold water.
2 Bring to the boil then simmer for 10 minutes.
3 Drain and transfer to a bowl, cover with a clean, dry tea towel and leave to stand for 4 minutes before serving.

TOP TIP Covering the hot, cooked rice with a tea towel and leaving it to stand dries the rice slightly and makes it fluff up.

SAAG ALOO

POINTS

per recipe: 2½   per serving: 2½

ⓥ Ⓥɢ *Serves 1*

Preparation and cooking time: 20
minutes
Calories per serving: 155
Freezing: not recommended

A spinach and potato dish to use as an accompaniment instead of rice, but which also makes a delightful vegetarian curry on its own.

low-fat cooking spray
1 medium onion, sliced
115 g (4 oz) fresh baby spinach
200 g (7 oz) potatoes, cooked and cubed
2.5 cm (1-inch) piece of fresh root
ginger, grated
1 medium green chilli, de-seeded and
chopped finely
1 teaspoon medium-strength curry
powder
1 teaspoon poppy seeds
salt and freshly ground black pepper

1 Heat a non-stick pan and spray with the low-fat cooking spray. Stir-fry the onion for about 5 minutes until soft.
2 Add the remaining ingredients to the pan together with 2 tablespoons water. Stir until the spinach has wilted.
3 Heat gently until simmering, then cover the pan with a tight-fitting lid and cook for 3 minutes or until the potatoes have warmed through.
4 Season to taste then serve.

TOP TIP You could also add 1 chopped garlic clove in step 2.

Saag aloo:
The popular
restaurant side
dish for only
2½ points
per serving.

Chutneys and raita:
The ideal low-point
side dishes.

ROASTED TOMATO AND CHILLI CHUTNEY

POINTS

per recipe: 0	per serving: 0

Ⓥ Ⓥg *Serves 4*

Preparation and cooking time: 15 minutes

Calories per serving: 30

Freezing: not recommended

A wide variety of different chutneys are served with Indian food, but all fall into one of two categories – those that are preserved and those that are freshly prepared and which should be eaten soon after making. This is a delicious fresh chutney that will keep for 2–3 days in the fridge. Great served with poppadums (½ point each).

4 medium tomatoes, halved

1 medum red onion, cut into 8 wedges

1 tablespoon tomato purée

1 tablespoon lime juice

1 tablespoon tamarind paste

¼–½ teaspoon dried red chillies

1 Preheat the grill to high.

2 Place the tomatoes and onion on a baking sheet and grill for 5 minutes until starting to blacken. Then turn the pieces over and continue to grill for 5 minutes more.

3 Remove the blackened tomato skins and then chop the tomatoes and onion roughly and put in a bowl. Add the rest of the ingredients and mix well.

TOP TIP Store in a bowl covered with clingfilm.

FRESH MANGO CHUTNEY

POINTS

per recipe: 3	per serving: 1

Ⓥ Ⓥg *Serves 4*

Preparation time: 15 minutes + 1 hour chilling

Calories per serving: 55

Freezing: not recommended

This is a fresh, spicy side dish to serve with curries.

2 medium fresh mangoes, stoned, peeled and diced

1 medium red chilli, chopped finely

a pinch of cumin seeds

1 Mix all the ingredients together in a bowl. Cover the bowl and chill for 1 hour before serving.

VARIATION Add 2 tablespoons chopped fresh mint leaves for extra taste but no extra points.

CUCUMBER RAITA

POINTS

per recipe: 2	per serving: ½

Ⓥ *Serves 4*

Preparation time: 10 minutes + 20 minutes chilling

Calories per serving: 45

Freezing: not recommended

Raitas are fresh and simple yogurt-based accompaniments. They are cooling and delicious with any curry but particularly appreciated with the hot ones!

½ medium cucumber, diced finely

250 ml (9 fl oz) low-fat plain bio yogurt

1 tablespoon chopped fresh coriander leaves

salt and freshly ground black pepper

1 Mix all the ingredients together in a bowl and season to taste. Cover with clingfilm then chill in the fridge for 20 minutes before serving.

VARIATIONS Add 1 medium green chilli, chopped finely, to the ingredients.

Substitute the cucumber with chopped fresh mint leaves and a little crushed garlic.

OVEN-BAKED CHILLI CHIPS

POINTS

per recipe: 12	per serving: 3

Ⓥ Ⓥᵍ *Serves 4*
Preparation time: 5 minutes
Cooking time: 20 minutes
Calories per serving: 190
Freezing: not recommended

An excellent accompaniment to many curry dishes but particularly good with those containing fish.

1 teaspoon chilli powder
¹/₂ teaspoon cumin seeds
600 g (1 lb 5 oz) low-fat oven chips
salt and freshly ground black pepper

1 Preheat the oven to Gas Mark 8/ 230°C/450°F.
2 Place the seasonings and the chips in a large plastic bag and shake together so that the seasonings coat the chips.
3 Spread over a large baking sheet or two small baking sheets in a single layer and bake for 18–20 minutes.

Oven-baked chilli chips: Wow – these taste great!

BOMBAY-STYLE POTATOES

POINTS

per recipe: 3¹/₂	per serving: 2

Ⓥ Ⓥᵍ *Serves 2*
Preparation and cooking time: 20 minutes
Calories per serving: 125
Freezing: not recommended

Potatoes were not introduced to India until the 19th century – so this is another British-inspired favourite.

low-fat cooking spray
¹/₂ teaspoon black mustard seeds
1 small onion, chopped roughly
2 teaspoons medium-strength curry powder
200 g (7 oz) potatoes, cubed
2 tablespoons half-fat crème fraîche
salt and freshly ground black pepper
a few sprigs of fresh coriander, to garnish (optional)

1 Heat a non-stick pan and spray with the low-fat cooking spray. Stir-fry the mustard seeds until they begin to pop.
2 Add the onion and fry for about 5 minutes until soft.
3 Add the curry powder and potatoes to the pan together with 200 ml (7 fl oz) cold water. Heat gently until simmering, then cover the pan with a tight-fitting lid and cook for 10 minutes.
4 Remove the lid and cook for 2–3 minutes more to ensure that the potatoes are cooked through and that the sauce has reduced and thickened slightly.
5 Stir in the crème fraîche, season to taste, garnish with coriander, if using and then serve.

Bombay-style potatoes: Spice up potatoes on the side.

Vegetable pilau:
Ideal with
tomato and
coriander salad
and a chappati
on the side.

VEGETABLE PILAU

POINTS

per recipe: 16   per serving: 4

Ⓥ Ⓥᴳ *Serves 4*
Preparation and cooking time: 35 minutes
Calories per serving: 295
Freezing: not recommended

A simple but delicious rice and vegetable mixture.

250 g (9 oz) basmati rice
4 garlic cloves, crushed
2.5 cm (1-inch) piece of fresh root ginger, grated
4 cardamom pods, crushed slightly
2 teaspoons ground coriander
1 teaspoon chilli powder
¹/₂ teaspoon turmeric
2 heaped tablespoons peas
low-fat cooking spray
400 g (14 oz) zero-point mixed vegetables, diced or sliced finely e.g. red and green peppers, cauliflower florets, small brown mushrooms
2 heaped tablespoons sultanas
salt and freshly ground black pepper

1 Put the rice, garlic, ginger and all the spices into a pan and cover with water. Heat until boiling and then continue to cook for 10 minutes. Add the peas after 7 minutes.
2 Heat a non-stick pan and spray with the low-fat cooking spray. Stir-fry the vegetables for 3–4 minutes.
3 When the rice is cooked, rinse and drain it, and transfer to a serving dish. Cover the dish with a clean, dry tea towel and set aside for 3–4 minutes.
4 Stir the vegetables and sultanas into the rice mixture, season to taste then serve.

TOMATO AND CORIANDER SALAD

POINTS

per recipe: 0   per serving: 0

Ⓥ Ⓥᴳ *Serves 2*
Preparation time: 5 minutes + 20 minutes chilling
Calories per serving: 15
Freezing: not recommended

Tomato and coriander complement each other beautifully and this easily-made accompaniment can be served with any curried dish.

2 medium tomatoes, one divided into wedges; the other chopped finely
¹/₂ tablespoon chopped fresh coriander leaves
a pinch of chilli powder
a pinch of sugar
¹/₂ tablespoon lemon juice
salt and freshly ground black pepper

1. Mix all ingredients together in a bowl. Cover and chill for 20 minutes before serving.

CHAPPATIS

POINTS

per recipe: 8¹/₂   per serving: 1

Ⓥ Ⓥᴳ *Makes 9*
Preparation and cooking time: 20 minutes + resting
Calories per serving: 80
Freezing: recommended

Chappatis are traditional Indian breads and are made by cooking them very quickly on top of the stove so that the dough puffs up. As they are made without fat, they are an ideal accompaniment to a curry to help keep the points low.

175 g (6 oz) wholemeal flour, plus 25 g (1 oz) for rolling
salt
low-fat cooking spray

1 Place the wholemeal flour in a medium-size bowl and season with salt.
2 Make a well in the middle and pour in 125 ml (4 fl oz) cold water.
3 Using two fingers, gently stir the flour and water together. Form into a ball, but add more water as required (up to 125 ml/4 fl oz). Once all the flour has been incorporated, knead to a smooth dough.
4 Sprinkle with a few drops of water, cover with a clean, damp tea towel and set aside for 30 minutes.
5 Knead again, then divide into 9 equal-sized pieces.
6 Using the reserved flour, roll each piece out into thin circles about 15 cm (6 inches) wide.
7 Preheat a frying pan and spray with the low-fat cooking spray. Fry each chappati for 1 minute on each side.
8 Serve immediately or leave until cool before wrapping in clingfilm and freezing until required.

Passion fruit yogurt: This creamy dessert is the perfect end to a spicy meal.

desserts

You may not be familiar with Indian desserts which are often based around fruit, milk or yogurt. Ice cream, enjoyed by the Moghul emperors centuries before modern ice creams became popular, was much firmer in texture than it is now, and it was flavoured with fruit and nuts. This chapter contains some delightfully light desserts, which finish a spicy Indian meal perfectly.

PASSION FRUIT YOGURT

POINTS	
per recipe: 5	per serving: 1

 Serves 4
Preparation time: 10 minutes + 30 minutes marinating
Calories per serving: 80
Freezing: not recommended

This is a traditional Indian dessert – if you like the taste of saffron you will love it.

a pinch of saffron, soaked in 4 tablespoons warm skimmed milk for at least 30 minutes, soaking liquid reserved

400 ml (14 fl oz) 0% fat Greek-style natural yogurt

2 teaspoons icing sugar

6 passion fruit, halved

1 Put the saffron and its soaking liquid together with the yogurt and icing sugar in a bowl. Stir well to mix.
2 Add the pulp from four of the passion fruit and stir again.
3 Divide the mixture between four small serving bowls and serve with the remaining passion fruit pulp spooned over the top.

Indian ice cream:
The real thing!

TROPICAL SORBET

POINTS

| per recipe: 8 | per serving: 1½ |

Ⓥ Ⓥg   *Serves 6*
Preparation time: 15 minutes +
freezing + 50 minutes softening
Calories per serving: 90
Freezing: recommended

You can of make this with any
cartons of juice or juice drinks as
long as they have a minimum fruit
content of 40% and do not have
more than 50 calories per 100 ml and
only a trace of saturated fat.

6 tablespoons sugar
½ tablespoon lemon juice
1 egg white
450 ml carton of tropical fruit drink

1 Put the sugar, 5 tablespoons of
water and the lemon juice into a
small pan and heat gently until
boiling. Simmer for 3–4 minutes
until the mixture has reduced and
thickened slightly. Remove from the
heat and set aside to cool.
2 In a scrupulously clean bowl, whisk
the egg white until it forms stiff peaks.
3 Pour the sugar syrup and the tropical
fruit drink into a food processor or
liquidiser and whisk together.
4 Gently fold the egg white into the
mixture and then pour it into a lidded
plastic container and freeze.
5 After 1½ hours, remove it from the
freezer; stir through with a fork
to break up any lumps. Cover the
container again. Return to the freezer.
6 After another 1½ hours, repeat this
procedure then leave to freeze for at
least 8 hours or preferably overnight.
7 Transfer it from the freezer to the
fridge 40–50 minutes before use to
allow it to soften. Serve 2 medium
scoops each in individual bowls.

INDIAN ICE CREAM

POINTS

| per recipe: 17 | per serving: 4 |

Ⓥ   *Serves 4*
Preparation time: 10 minutes +
freezing + 50 minutes softening
Calories per serving: 305
Freezing: recommended

This lovely Indian ice cream, known
as kulfi, is traditionally made by a
long method of reducing full-fat
milk. This is a quicker alternative,
which uses a can of light condensed
milk.

410 g can of light condensed milk
30 g (1¼ oz) sugar
*2 cardamom pods, de-seeded, crushed
and ground; empty pods discarded*

1 Put all the ingredients into a food
processor or liquidiser, and whisk or
blend until well mixed.
2 Pour into a lidded plastic container
and freeze.
3 After 2 hours, remove from the
freezer; stir through with a fork to
break up any lumps. Cover the
container again. Return to the freezer.
4 After another 2 hours, repeat this
procedure then leave to freeze for at
least 8 hours or preferably overnight.
5 Transfer it from the freezer to the
fridge 45–50 minutes before serving
to allow it to soften. Serve 4 small
scoops per person.

Tropical sorbet:
Finish on a high
note for only
1½ points per
serving!

LEMON CHEESE
ICE CREAM

POINTS	
per recipe: 8½	per serving: 1½

Ⓥ Serves 6
Preparation time: 10 minutes +
freezing + 30 minutes softening
Calories per serving: 95
Freezing: recommended

250 ml (9 fl oz) skimmed milk
100 g (3½ oz) low-fat soft cheese
85 g (3 oz) caster sugar
grated zest and juice of 2 lemons

1 Put all the ingredients into a food
processor or liquidiser, and whisk or
blend until well mixed.
2 Pour into a lidded plastic container
and freeze.
3 After 1½ hours, remove it from
the freezer. Stir through with a fork
to break up any lumps. Cover the
container again. Return to the freezer.
4 After another 1½ hours, repeat this
procedure then leave to freeze for
8 hours or preferably overnight.
5 Transfer to the fridge 30 minutes
before serving to allow it to soften.
Serve 2 medium scoops per person.

**Lemon cheese
ice cream:
Creamy and
satisfying.**

SPICED FRUIT
SALAD

POINTS	
per recipe: 5½	per serving: 1½

Ⓥ Ⓥᵍ Serves 4
Preparation time: 10 minutes +
chilling
Calories per serving: 100
Freezing: not recommended

This fresh fruit salad tastes even
better the day after it is made, so it
makes an ideal dinner party dessert.
Make it the day before you have
guests, then just take it straight from
the fridge when required.

large slice of fresh pineapple
(225 g/8 oz), cubed
½ fresh stoned mango (225 g/8 oz),
peeled and cubed
a medium slice of canteloupe melon
(200 g/7 oz) de-seeded, peeled and
cubed
½ small bunch of seedless grapes
(50 g/1¾ oz)
2 pieces of stem ginger (30 g/1¼ oz),
washed and sliced thinly
1 teaspoon sugar
juice of 1 lime
mango slices with skin, to decorate
(optional)

1 Place all fruit ingredients and the
stem ginger in a serving bowl.
2 Put the sugar and lime juice in a
bowl and make up to 75 ml (2½ fl oz)
with water. Stir until the sugar has
dissolved.
3 Pour the lime syrup over the fruit,
cover and chill in the fridge for 1
hour, or preferably overnight.
4 Serve in bowls with the mango
slices for more colour and texture,
if desired.

Spiced fruit salad: A refreshing and attractive dessert; only 1½ points per serving.

**Lime sherbert:
Enjoy this
popular Indian
drink for no
points at all!**

LIME SHERBET

 Serves 4

Preparation time: 10 minutes
Calories per serving: 5
Freezing: not recommended

In India, sherbets are served as long, cool drinks. This is a great drink to serve with an Indian meal or as a refreshing drink on a hot summer's day.

---

juice of 4 limes
3 tablespoons of low-calorie granulated sweetener
mint leaves, to garnish

---

1 Put the lime juice and sweetener in a bowl and stir together until the sweetener has dissolved.
2 Half-fill four tall glasses with ice-cubes or crushed ice.
3 Divide the sweetened lime juice between the glasses and top up each one with iced water.
4 Stir the contents of each glass, garnish with mint leaves then serve.

PINEAPPLE SORBET

 Serves 6

Preparation time: 20 minutes +
6 hours freezing
Calories per serving: 100
Freezing: recommended

This sorbet tastes best when freshly made.

---

6 tablespoons caster sugar
½ tablespoon lemon juice
1 egg white
425 g can of crushed pineapple in natural juice

---

1 Put the sugar, 5 tablespoons of water and the lemon juice into a small pan and heat gently until boiling. Simmer for 3–4 minutes until the mixture has reduced and thickened slightly. Remove from the heat and set aside to cool.
2 In a scrupulously clean bowl, whisk the egg white until it forms stiff peaks.
3 Pour the sugar syrup and the crushed pineapple with its juice into a food processor or liquidiser and whisk together.
4 Gently fold the egg white into the mixture then pour it into a lidded plastic container and freeze.
5 After 1½ hours, remove from the freezer. Stir through with a fork to break up any lumps. Cover the container again. Return to the freezer.
6 After another 1½ hours, repeat this procedure then leave to freeze for 2–3 hours until almost frozen.
7 Either serve straight away or freeze overnight. If serving from frozen, transfer it from the freezer to the fridge 20 minutes before use to allow it to soften. Serve scoops in individual bowls.

BANANA YOGURT ICE

 Serves 4

Preparation time: 10 minutes +
freezing + 50 minutes softening
Calories per serving: 175
Freezing: recommended

This recipe is best when made with very ripe bananas – it is an ideal way to use up bananas whose skins are turning black.

---

300 ml (10 fl oz) low-fat plain bio yogurt
3 medium, very ripe bananas
40 g (1½ oz) sugar
2 tablespoons skimmed milk powder

---

1 Put all the ingredients into a food processor or liquidiser, and whisk or blend until well mixed.
2 Pour into a lidded plastic container and freeze.
3 After 2 hours, remove it from the freezer and stir through with a fork to break up any lumps. Cover the container again and return to the freezer.
4 After another 2 hours, repeat this procedure then leave to freeze for at least 8 hours or preferably overnight.
5 Transfer it from the freezer to the fridge 45–50 minutes before serving to allow it to soften. Serve 2 medium scoops per person in individual bowls.